Cross-Cultural Existentialism

Also available from Bloomsbury

Comparative Philosophy without Borders, edited by Arindam Chakrabarti and Ralph Weber
Comparative Studies in Asian and Latin American Philosophies, edited by Stephanie Rivera Berruz and Leah Kalmanson
Differences in Identity in Philosophy and Religion, edited by Sarah Flavel and Russell Re Manning
Faith and Reason in Continental and Japanese Philosophy, by Takeshi Morisato
Imagination: Cross-Cultural Philosophical Analyses, edited by Hans-Georg Moeller and Andrew Whitehead

Cross-Cultural Existentialism

On the Meaning of Life in Asian and Western Thought

Leah Kalmanson

BLOOMSBURY ACADEMIC
LONDON • NEW YORK • OXFORD • NEW DELHI • SYDNEY

BLOOMSBURY ACADEMIC
Bloomsbury Publishing Plc
50 Bedford Square, London, WC1B 3DP, UK
1385 Broadway, New York, NY 10018, USA
29 Earlsfort Terrace, Dublin 2, Ireland

BLOOMSBURY, BLOOMSBURY ACADEMIC and the Diana logo
are trademarks of Bloomsbury Publishing Plc

First published in Great Britain 2021
This paperback edition published in 2022

Copyright © Leah Kalmanson, 2021

Leah Kalmanson has asserted her right under the Copyright,
Designs and Patents Act, 1988, to be identified as Author of this work.

For legal purposes the Acknowledgments on p.vi constitute
an extension of this copyright page.

Cover image by Christopher Chiavetta, Green Key, 2019 (acrylic on paper, 12" x 12").
Photo courtesy of Alyss Vernon, Olson-Larsen Galleries (West Des Moines, Iowa).

All rights reserved. No part of this publication may be reproduced or transmitted in any form or by any means, electronic or mechanical, including photocopying, recording, or any information storage or retrieval system, without prior permission in writing from the publishers.

Bloomsbury Publishing Plc does not have any control over, or responsibility for, any third-party websites referred to or in this book. All internet addresses given in this book were correct at the time of going to press. The author and publisher regret any inconvenience caused if addresses have changed or sites have
ceased to exist, but can accept no responsibility for any such changes.

A catalogue record for this book is available from the British Library.

Library of Congress Cataloging-in-Publication Data
Names: Kalmanson, Leah, 1977- author.
Title: Cross-cultural existentialism : on the meaning of life in Asian and Western thought / Leah Kalmanson.
Description: London ; New York : Bloomsbury Academic, 2020. | Includes bibliographical references and index. | Summary: "Expanding the scope of existential discourse beyond the Western tradition, this book engages Asian philosophies to reassess vital questions of life's purpose, death's imminence, and our capacity for living meaningfully in conditions of uncertainty. Inspired by European existentialism in theory, the book explores concrete techniques for existential practice via the philosophies of East Asia. The investigation begins with the provocative existential writings of twentieth-century Korean Buddhist nun Kim Iryop, who asserts that meditative concentration conducts a potent energy outward throughout the entire karmic network, enabling the radical transformation of our shared existential conditions. Understanding her claim requires a study of East Asian traditions more broadly. Considering practices as diverse as Song-dynasty Chinese views on mental cultivation, Buddhist merit-making ceremonies, the ritual memorization and recitation of texts, and Yijing divination, the book concludes by advocating a speculative turn. This 'speculative existentialism' counters the suspicion toward metaphysics characteristic of twentieth-century European existential thought and, at the same time, advances a program for action. It is not a how-to guide for living, but rather a philosophical methodology that takes seriously the power of mental cultivation to transform the meaning of the life that we share"– Provided by publisher.
Identifiers: LCCN 2020020646 (print) | LCCN 2020020647 (ebook) | ISBN 9781350140011 (hardback) | ISBN 9781350140028 (ebook) | ISBN 9781350140035 (epub)
Subjects: LCSH: Existentialism. Classification: LCC B819 .K235 2020 (print) | LCC B819 (ebook) | DDC 181–dc23
LC record available at https://lccn.loc.gov/2020020646
LC ebook record available at https://lccn.loc.gov/2020020647

ISBN:	HB:	978-1-3501-4001-1
	PB:	978-1-3502-0563-5
	ePDF:	978-1-3501-4002-8
	eBook:	978-1-3501-4003-5

Typeset by Integra Software Services Pvt. Ltd.

To find out more about our authors and books visit www.bloomsbury.com
and sign up for our newsletters.

Contents

Acknowledgments	vi
Introduction: Toward a Speculative Existentialism	1
1 Meaningful Dilemmas: Existential Inquiry in the Western Tradition	17
2 The Creation of New Values, Part I: Karmic Transformations	41
3 The Creation of New Values, Part II: Cosmic Correspondences	69
4 Rituals for Existential Re-habituation	95
Conclusion: Return to Inner Experience	129
Notes	143
References	168
Index	182

Acknowledgments

This book would not have been possible without the advice, critical feedback, and support of the members of my writing group, Aaron Creller (University of North Florida), Andrew Lambert (College of Staten Island), and Sarah Mattice (University of North Florida). Their positive influence on the manuscript cannot be overstated; all deficiencies are my own. I would like to thank Drake University for granting the sabbatical leave that enabled this project in its early stages. I would also like to thank my parents, Neil and Mary Kalmanson, who were so excited to hear I was working on a book that they began telling people about it before I'd actually written anything, which prompted me to get started. Finally, I am grateful beyond words to my husband Christopher Chiavetta, who was never bothered by the piles of books on the kitchen table or the Chinese-language flash cards taped to the walls, and who provided the artwork that I am so proud to have on the cover.

Image Acknowledgment
Cover image by Christopher Chiavetta, *Green Key*, 2019 (acrylic on paper, 12 x 12 inches). Photo courtesy of Alyss Vernon, Olson-Larsen Galleries (West Des Moines, Iowa).

Introduction: Toward a Speculative Existentialism

The sovereign desire of beings is what is beyond being. Anguish is the feeling of danger related to this inexhaustible expectation.
—Georges Bataille[1]

Sometimes it boggles the mind that death is still a mystery. If philosophical "progress" is judged by traction gained on that particular problem, then we cannot be said to have gotten very far. Yet our impending mortality never fails to stir up opinions. Of course, we can ignore the question of death, or call it absurd, or accept the inevitable and move on—but any serious inquiry into the meaning of life must give due credit to the persistent uncertainty of our final destination as a motivating factor behind common existential concerns.

As will be evident in what follows, my own concerns tend toward ultimate questions: the origins of existence, the nature of sentient life, the mystery of death. Facing the sheer quantity of all these uncertainties, my work in the present book grows out of a strong belief that effective existential philosophy must be a practice as much as it is a theory. This belief is not unique—European existentialists on the whole take seriously the idea that their philosophies are meant to be *lived*. However, as seen in Pierre Hadot's (1922–2010) research on ancient Greek and Roman philosophers, academics today have lost the specific techniques for philosophical practice that were once central to the discipline.[2] In a telling comment, Hadot concludes his discussion of Greek and Roman "spiritual exercises" by saying: "Not until Nietzsche,

Bergson, and existentialism does philosophy consciously return to being a concrete attitude, a way of life and of seeing the world."[3] Undoubtedly the attention to concrete experience and everyday life is a key feature of existential philosophy, but I find little evidence of explicit instructions for "spiritual exercises" in the style of the ancient Greeks and Romans in existential writings.[4] As a result, without a repertoire of practical strategies for existential re-*habituation*, certain dilemmas of Western thought repeatedly reemerge at crucial junctures in philosophical studies on the question of meaning in life.

In particular, a problematic understanding of subjective interiority—the inner life of the mind—remains influential, despite explicit theoretical moves taken in existential thought to reject, subvert, or circumvent subject–object dualism and the metaphysical picture of the self that accompanies it. For this reason, the present exercise in cross-cultural existentialism looks to East Asian discourses that approach the phenomenon of subjective interiority differently. Such traditions not only include robust theoretical articulations of the nature of inner life but also offer a range of practical techniques for mental cultivation, self-transformation, and existential realization. Some of these techniques, such as meditation, have already received attention in contemporary cross-cultural philosophical literature; but many of the practices that we will explore have not been taken up within philosophy and certainly not within existentialism, such as Buddhist merit-making ceremonies, the ritual memorization and recitation of texts, and divination via the *Yijing* (易經) or *Book of Changes*.

Along with such practices, we find what has been called a "microcosm-macrocosm" model of the relations between humans and their environments.[5] This model assumes that fundamental structures are isomorphic across myriad phenomena, from the smallest scale to the largest, such that transformations at one level can potentially reverberate up and down by means of corresponding systems.

As such, this model reframes the distinction between the inner mind and the external world and thereby undermines a number of binaries that have long shaped Western thought, such as realism and idealism, rationalism and empiricism, and materialism and vitalism. More provocatively, it challenges assumptions about the dividing line between the natural and the so-called supernatural—a line that either explicitly or implicitly limits what contemporary existentialism will entertain as a reasonable or plausible answer to the question of meaning in life. In other words, when we ask about what is *really* meaningful, a lot depends on what we mean by *reality*.

Chapter 1: Is Anything "Really" Meaningful?

This book entertains a simple but provocative question: What if mental experience is not unique to the brain or otherwise housed "within" the skull? Reading a wide array of texts in East Asian philosophy, we find the pervasive assumption that mental energies reside both inside and outside the body, that such energies can interact with each other, and that they in turn can interact with other types of energies in the material environment.[6] How might these assumptions about the character of mental life affect existential inquiry?

As noted above, most contemporary philosophers reject the idea of a metaphysical subject—historically, phenomenology and existentialism in Europe, as well as analytic philosophy in the Anglo-American world, all arose as reactions against metaphysical speculation. For example, phenomenology attends to the minutia of immediate experience without making claims as to the nature of the "self" or the metaphysical status of the subject. Likewise, contemporary analytic philosophy looks into the relationship between the mind and the brain from numerous perspectives, including philosophy of mind, philosophy of science, and the more recent field of neurophilosophy.

None of these discourses on either side of the continental–analytic divide conceive of mental experiences as the kinds of energies routinely mentioned in East Asian traditions. The present project exploits the simple fact that, in rejecting the metaphysical subject, Western philosophy has mostly rejected one or more of its *own* versions of that subject (i.e., Plato's rational charioteer of the body, the Christian soul, Descartes's "thinking thing," and so forth). What if we return to speculative philosophy for the sake of considering views on mental life that do not reduce to one of these Western versions?

The investigation begins in the first chapter with a recent debate between two prominent American philosophers over the question of meaning in life, in which underlying assumptions about the subject–object divide show up particularly clearly. Their disagreement concerns whether, objectively speaking, existence has meaning, or if instead meaningfulness is merely a quality of subjective experience. As we will see, these are the only two options entertained: either meaning exists "out there" somehow, independently of us; or meaning is a figment of our minds. The first position seems to commit us to a degree of realism or perhaps religion (i.e., the idea that meaning exists on its own, like a Platonic form or a God-given fact), while the second seems to resign us to nihilism in the end (i.e., the world at large, regardless of the human experience of it, remains meaningless). The remainder of the chapter contextualizes this dilemma within the history of realist–idealist debates in Western thought. In the eighteenth and nineteenth centuries, we see philosophy stumped again and again by the limits of subjective experience, unable to speculate about what might lie beyond, whether this refers to metaphysical realities or simply the nature of objects presumed to be external to the mind. We trace the impact of this dilemma on twentieth-century existential philosophy, from the work of Simone de Beauvoir, to the related writings of phenomenologists, and through recent critics who have proclaimed phenomenology dead.

In particular, emerging fields such as speculative realism, new materialism, and object-oriented ontology all criticize, in different ways, the phenomenological picture of subjective interiority.[7] Many of these recent turns in continental philosophy and critical theory are indebted to the speculative philosophy of Alfred North Whitehead (1861–1947),[8] whose work, as Steven Shaviro points out, has been overshadowed by that of the existential phenomenologist Martin Heidegger (1889–1976), in terms of influence on twentieth-century and contemporary continental thought.[9]

The "speculative existentialism" developed in this book is inspired by these recent critical turns in Western discourse but generally seeks to ground itself in close readings of Asian philosophical material with a minimum of comparative exposition. As said above, by "speculative," I mean that this work pushes back against the resistance to metaphysics characteristic of contemporary phenomenology and existentialism. But, I should also clarify, so-called metaphysics itself is a category constructed by and within the parameters of Western intellectual history, and so the extent to which the East Asian material this book will engage should be called "metaphysical" is debatable.[10] Rather than argue over the use of the term, I aim instead to read East Asian philosophical claims about the nature of reality in their own words, with reference to the original languages wherever possible,[11] in order to see how these claims can change our understanding of the practices central to human meaning-making.

In particular, by enabling us to challenge assumptions about the parameters of subjective experience, East Asian discourses help us redefine "speculation" itself *not* as the interior ruminations of a subject looking out on the world but rather as a *dynamic activity that transforms both selves and their environments*. Eiho Baba has recently argued that the word usually translated as "perception" (*zhijue* 知覺) in Song-dynasty (960–1279) Chinese texts "is not a passive 'seeing' as it were, of a predetermined reality, but a participatory determination, if not artistic production of the world through cultivated skills of appreciation and realization."[12] As this shows, the Chinese terminology helps to push the notion of speculation in a dynamic direction—rather than reflecting states of mind, modes of awareness, or theoretical attitudes, the Chinese terms for knowing and perceiving all indicate the creative, mutually transformative interplay between human consciousness and the world. A "speculative existentialism" is a trans-egoic activity, not only an intellectual theory.

Chapters 2 and 3: On the Question of Meaning-Making in East Asian Thought

Issues of translation and terminology figure prominently in any cross-cultural philosophical venture. Before the terms "philosophy" and "religion" were translated into Asian languages, early encounters with European Christians show East Asian scholars and officials attempting to classify foreigners according to local categories.[13] They drew on precedents related to discourses surrounding the reception of the Indian dharma or "teachings" in China vis-à-vis the indigenous traditions of *daojia/daojiao* (道家/道教), or Daoism, and *rujia* (儒家), or the "scholarly lineage" that has come to be called "Confucianism" in the West.

Confucianism is a misleading term that suggests the historical figure of "Confucius" (Kongzi 孔子, 551–479 BCE) was the founder of a religious, or perhaps philosophical, movement. In fact, the tradition known in Chinese as *rujia* well predates the life of Kongzi, and Kongzi himself denies being an innovator.[14] Rather, he was a member of the "lineage" or "family" (*jia* 家) of the *ru* (儒), a term better translated as "scholar" or "literati." The *ru* were members of China's educated elite: they were most often employed as educators or government officials, they were versed in classic philosophical and literary texts, and they were qualified to preside over various state rites and civic ceremonies as well as the rituals performed at ancestral shrines. Throughout this book, I use the alternative English terms "Ruism" and "Ruists" to refer to the tradition and its members. This use of Ruism also better conveys the sense in which the standards of practice for the "scholars" or "literati" might be applied cross-culturally. The historian Clinton Godart has commented: "When speaking about 'Asian philosophy,' the burden of proof is placed on the Asian traditions. Questions are posed such as 'was Confucianism philosophy,' not 'was Hegel a Confucianist' or 'did he complete the Way?' Thus Westernization has created a cultural imbalance of categories and representations."[15] My terminological choices in this book are often aimed at correcting this imbalance. For example, it may sound strange to ask whether Hegel was a "Confucianist" but less so to ask whether he was a good "scholar" by Ruist standards. In this sense, along with Ruism, I use the term "dharma" to speak broadly of Buddhism and its teachings related to enlightenment or awakening ("buddha"[16] means "awakened one").

In general, I will be treating both Ruism and dharma as flexible categories whose standards for practice can be applied across cultures much as we already apply the standards definitive of "philosophy" and "religion."[17] This captures the precise sense in which my work is in "cross-cultural existentialism." Compared to other fields within philosophy, existentialism has been marked by diverse voices, including scholarship in the African diaspora, such as Black existentialism and Africana critical theory, as well as in Latin America, and in Asia. My commitment to a methodological intervention via Ruist and Buddhist scholarly practices is indebted to this boundary-pushing and boundary-crossing heritage of existentialism as a field.

With all this in mind, I seek in the second chapter to understand the provocative existential writings of the twentieth-century Korean Buddhist nun Kim Wonju (1896–1971), dharma name Iryŏp,[18] who asserts that meditative concentration is not simply a private affair but instead conducts a potent energy throughout the entire karmic network in which all beings are located, enabling the radical transformation of our shared existential condition. To understand what she could possibly mean will require philosophical speculation. The key point—the reason why this existential project must be speculative—is that a cluster of broadly Buddhist and Ruist theoretical assumptions about the nature of mind and reality underlie Iryŏp's understanding of the efficacy of her meditation practices. I would do a disservice to her thought were I to pluck such practices out of this theoretical context and thereby avoid engaging her own philosophical sensibilities.[19]

Buddhist views on emptiness and impermanence have already inspired a number of major works in comparative philosophy on existential themes, especially through engagement with the writings of Friedrich Nietzsche (1844–1900).[20] That said, in order to contextualize Iryŏp's account of the trans-egoic power of meditation, the second chapter pursues an alternative but complimentary track, taking inspiration not from the Buddhist analysis of emptiness but from everyday practices related to the production and exchange of karmic merit via various ritual enactments. A study of this karmic economy helps to explain the exchange of energy underlying Iryŏp's seemingly fantastical account of enlightened beings as creators of worlds and her conviction that the "inner" experience of the meditator's mind reverberates well beyond the bounds of the body.[21]

In the end, we find that her provocative views on meditation require a broader look at the relation of Buddhism to other philosophical traditions in East Asia, especially Song-dynasty Ruist thought, which began in China and spread as a scholarly movement into Korea and Japan. As will become clear, my book is ultimately about the radical existential vision of Ruism, a tradition that has, in general, received less attention than Buddhism in comparative existential work. And, accordingly, in this book I approach Iryŏp as a Ruist thinker as much as a Buddhist, although this may at first seem counterintuitive, given her progressive politics and feminist commitments. But Iryŏp is a syncretic philosopher, whose deep ties to Christianity (her father was a Methodist preacher) give her a unique perspective on the philosophies of East Asia as well as the religious crises that inform European existentialism. And syncretism is a key feature of the three major East Asian traditions in general—Buddhism, Ruism, and Daoism—which are marked by a long history of mutual influence and accommodation. Given all this, Iryŏp's idiosyncratic take on Buddhist philosophy, which cannot be understood apart from the broader East Asian philosophical assumptions that inform it, is a productive starting point for this existential investigation.

Next, in the third chapter, I reexamine Iryŏp's account of meditation in light of East Asian theories on the cosmology and ontology of *qi* (氣), which has roots in China's earliest literature but comes to the fore as a subject of philosophical speculation among the Ruists of the Song (960–1279) and Ming (1368–1644) dynasties. A *qi*-based philosophy offers a plausible framework for explaining *why* Buddhist practices are existentially transformative and, ultimately, *how* activities at the microcosmic level of human awareness (e.g., meditation) have efficacious reach into the surrounding community, environment, and even cosmos.

The term *qi* (氣) has been translated into English variously as "vital stuff,"[22] "psychophysical stuff,"[23] and "lively material."[24] As theorized by the Song and Ming philosophers, anything that exists is some form of *qi*, whether it is condensed and palpable, as in physical objects, or dispersed and ethereal, as in the spiritual energies of the human mind. The study of *qi* was simultaneously the study of the corresponding term *li* (理), which refers to the "structures," "principles," or "patterns" observable in *qi*'s actions and tendencies.[25] Through their investigations into *qi* and *li*, the Song–Ming philosophers posed questions such as: Given the creative potency of *qi*, why does it configure itself into the world as we know it, as opposed to other possible configurations? Does a certain order (*li*) govern the behavior of *qi*? If so, how do we apprehend and enact this order? Some philosophers assert that *li* has no independent existence but only describes the tendencies inherent in *qi* itself. Others seem to suggest that *li* is a governing principle that does exist on its own and can be studied as such. Many others take a position somewhere in between, speaking of the mutual dependence of the two terms. As the famed Song-dynasty scholar Zhu Xi (1130–1200) says, "In the cosmos there has never been any psychophysical stuff without structure nor any structure without psychophysical stuff."[26]

Above all, *li* refers to the correspondences that obtain between various microcosmic and macrocosmic levels of reality. Zhu Xi himself took inspiration from the opening passage of the *Daxue* (大學) or "Great Learning" section of China's classical text the *Liji* (禮記) or *Book of Rites*, which gives a clear picture of the mutually transformative relations between microcosmic and macrocosmic structures:

> The ancients, in wishing to illuminate luminous power in the world, first brought good order to their own states. Wanting to bring good order to their states, they first regulated their households. Wanting to regulate their households, they first cultivated themselves. Wanting to cultivate themselves, they first corrected their minds. Wanting to correct their minds, they first made their intentions sincere. Wanting to make their intentions sincere, they first extended their knowledge. Extending knowledge consists in investigating things. Investigate things, and knowledge is extended. Extend knowledge, and intention becomes sincere. Make intention sincere, and the mind becomes correct. Correct the mind, and the self is cultivated. Cultivate the self, and the household is regulated. Regulate the household, and the state is brought to good order. Bring good order to the state, and the whole world will be at peace. From the ruler down to ordinary people, all must regard the cultivation of the self as the root.[27]

A structural isomorphism is evident between these different levels named in the *Daxue*, which reflects what sinologist Jana Rŏsker has described as "the structural compatibility of mind and the external world."[28] In other words, there is a basic compatibility between the heart-mind (*xin* 心) of the sage and conditions in the surrounding environment, both social and physical. An individual is certainly impacted by her environment, but at the same time she can exert a strong and charismatic influence over the world around her.

The recursive behavior of *qi*, or its ability to interact with itself in its different phases to produce increasingly complex manifestations of structure (*li*), is the key feature that enables the *Daxue*'s program of personal, social, and environmental cultivation. In Ruist terms, the sage (*shengren* 聖人) is the person who has put in the time and effort toward self-cultivation that enables her influence over surrounding conditions. Self-cultivation is often described as a process of manipulating the *qi* of the heart-mind to achieve stillness (*jing* 靜), numinosity (*ling* 靈), and spiritual clarity (*shenming* 神明).[29] In contrast, petty or "small" people (*xiaoren* 小人) fail to attain access beyond the perspective of their own limited awareness. They barely understand themselves, let alone the outside world and other people; their *qi* remains turbid and cloudy.

The general framework of *qi*-philosophy provides crucial context for understanding Kim Iryŏp's views on meditation discussed in the second chapter. As Kim claimed, meditation is not simply a private experience but an efficacious practice that conducts transformative energy into the surrounding world. Here, her language seems to reflect overarching East Asian views on *qi* as much as her Buddhist training. In fact, the three philosophical traditions of Ruism, Daoism, and Buddhism converge on a key point that has far-reaching implications for our existential engagement with the question of meaning-making: namely, these traditions all agree that a creative power issues forth from the well-cultivated heart-mind of a sage or enlightened being.

At this point we can better appreciate the resources that the Chinese tradition brings to the project of speculative philosophy: if we are looking for a mode of speculation that grants us access to reality beyond the constraints of the ordinary subjective perspective, then this intermixing of internal and external—this resonant attunement of mind-*qi* through the apprehension of *li*—is speculation par excellence. Issues such as solipsism, subjective idealism, and other apparent dilemmas of subjectivity, which have so frequently thwarted philosophical and existential inquiry in the West, may turn out to be—no offence—only a function of limited (*xiao* 小) thinking.

Power, Structure, and Meaning

In the engagement with Buddhism and Ruism in the second and third chapters, we look not only for theoretical insights but for concrete practices aimed at enacting this transformed and transformative sage-consciousness under real-world conditions. In addition to the terms *qi* and *li* above, a third Chinese philosophical concept becomes important for articulating these practices: *de* (德), often defined as "virtue" or "power," is associated with forces of nature and the momentum of natural cycles, the human capacity for radical self-transformation, and the moral charisma of exemplary political leaders.

The relation of structure (*li*) to power (*de*) in Chinese thought points toward potential interventions in contemporary continental philosophy and critical theory, which have what we might call a deflationary account of subjective agency. In other words, the subject is fully an effect of social power, produced and sustained through a network of interlocking structures. The philosopher and sociologist Maurizio Lazzarato succinctly expresses this general trend in his recent study of capitalism and the construction of subjectivity:

It is never an individual who thinks, never an individual who creates. An individual who thinks and creates does so within a network of institutions (schools, theaters, museums, libraries, etc.), technologies (books, electronic networks, computers, etc.), and sources of public and private financing; an individual immersed in traditions of thought and aesthetic practices—engulfed in a circulation of signs, ideas, and tasks—that force him or her to think and create.[30]

This constructivist account of subjectivity is indebted to thinkers such as Judith Butler and Michel Foucault, who themselves owe much to Friedrich Nietzsche's hyperbolic declarations that the subject is a fiction and all so-called truth claims are power-grabs in disguise.[31]

Many feminist philosophers aligned with the continental tradition (and I count myself here) have wondered whether selves entirely constituted by power relations are not thereby determined by those relations. Various creative solutions have been suggested[32] (and Butler's own account of agency grows more robust over time), but still the possibilities for self-determination in the constructivist framework all seem like small cracks in the wall of the larger and dominating power structures that determine subjective life.

Reflecting on this situation, Foucault develops toward the end of his career an interest in Hadot's work and the forgotten practices of Western philosophy mentioned above, especially Stoic and early Christian practices of self-cultivation. As he writes: "Perhaps I've insisted too much on the technology of domination and power. I am more and more interested in the interaction between oneself and others in the technologies of individual domination, the history of how an individual acts upon himself, in the technology of self."[33] In this later work, we see a more optimistic and possibly liberatory side of social constructivist theory—we are not simply at the mercy of larger social forces but can play an active role in the construction of both self and society. Exploring this liberatory potential, Foucault investigates Stoic techniques for self-reflection, self-assessment, and self-control, hinging on various uses of meditation, abstinence, fasting, and so forth. He comments: "In the culture of the Stoics, their function is to establish and test the independence of the individual with regard to the external world."[34]

Here, in this moment of optimism, we again see familiar philosophical territory—i.e., the split between inner experience and outer world. In Foucault's studies of both Stoic practices and Christian ones (such as confession and self-renunciation), we see this conflict between inner and outer, or between spirit and matter, marking an uneasy relationship between the rational soul and the world and the body that it occupies. Indeed, all such Greek, Roman, and Christian practices give us a picture of the self that is indebted to the very metaphysics of (spiritual) subject and (material) object that existential philosophy rejects. Overall, if we are looking for a systematic account of daily practices, both personal and social, that relate to enacting the vision of trans-egoic meaning-making expressed in existential theory, we will not find it within existential writings themselves.

My turn to East Asian sources, then, marks a sharp exit from the binaries that covertly, or overtly, shape discourse about the human condition in continental philosophy and critical theory. Nietzsche's call for the creation of new values still echoes—he was always optimistic about the constructive force of his philosophy—but no one has yet agreed upon what this value-creation requires.[35] I want to take thinkers such as Foucault, Butler, and especially Nietzsche out of their home territory and resituate them in *Qi*-based philosophy, where the operation of structure and the efficacy of self-cultivation speak to the fundamental permeability of "inner" and "outer."

Chapter 4: Building a *Qi*-Based Existential Vocabulary

Although this is not a book about Friedrich Nietzsche, his ideas appear at key junctures throughout the work. As we investigate the sage's power to forge new values—values that are not simply the projections of subjective meaning onto the world—I remain indebted to Nietzsche and to cross-cultural philosophers who have engaged him.[36] The great comparative philosopher of Nietzsche, Graham Parkes, tells us:

> One can love the world if, like Zarathustra, one has experienced it as all entwined and "perfect"—when as a streaming of will to power one streams with the "streaming and counter-streaming, and ebb and flood" of the ocean of energies that is the world as will to power; when like the Confucian thinker Mencius one has "cultivated one's flood-like energies" so that they "fill the space between heaven and earth" and harmonize with "the Way" of the world; when like the Daoist sage one has accumulated one's powers (*de*) and emptied one's mind so that one's activity flows from the Way of heaven and earth and the myriad processes; or when one reaches that "fundamental level," as Nishitani puts it, "where the world moves at one with the self, and the self moves at one with the world."[37]

Amplifying these resonances between Nietzsche's work and a range of East Asian philosophies, the fourth chapter looks to build, in a broad sense, a *qi*-based existential vocabulary. Mindful of Nietzsche's call for a new health—"the *great health*"[38]—speculative existentialism investigates concrete techniques for "daily renewal" (*rixin* 日新) and "ceaseless vitality" (*shengsheng bu xi* 生生不息), seeking to move past the old existentialist values of anxiety, absurdity, and alienation, to imagine new ones, rooted in the daily discipline and balanced nourishment of philosophical practice.

The small set of terms I select—namely, solicitude (*you* 憂), seriousness (*jing* 敬), stillness (*jing* 靜), sincerity (*cheng* 誠), and spontaneity (*ziran* 自然)—would certainly not be labeled "existentialist" anywhere within East Asian traditions themselves. But, in turn, each idea helps us to reframe the vocabulary of Western existentialism: solicitude instead of anxiety, seriousness instead of absurdity, stillness instead of alienation, and sincerity and spontaneity in place of authenticity and freedom. Through this exercise, I do not seek to answer Western existential questions so much as to gain new perspective on the habitual modes of thinking that sustain those lines of inquiry and consider possibilities for re-*habituation*. Indeed, all of the terms I choose are associated with one or more practices, be these scholarly methods, contemplative techniques, or closer to what Western discourses would call religious rituals. In the end, my goal is not to articulate speculative existentialism as a how-to guide for meaningful living but rather an existential methodology that takes seriously the power of self-cultivation and, accordingly, recognizes the necessity of committing daily to the practices that develop such power.

By the time the book concludes, we find that we have slowly redefined the contested category of "inner experience." Rather than the phenomenological interiority indebted to a range of metaphysical and anti-metaphysical positions, a *qi*-based philosophy explains inner experience in terms of turbid and calm mental energies, which are not categorically differentiated from bodily forms and physical matter in general. The deepest sense of "inner experience," on a *qi*-based model, refers to the capacity of the heart-mind to relax into its primordial and undifferentiated state through various scholarly, ritual, and contemplative practices. By relinquishing accumulated mental structures, the heart-mind refreshes itself and replenishes its fundamental creative potency, making possible an existential re-habituation that speaks to the productive power of speculative thought.

1

Meaningful Dilemmas: Existential Inquiry in the Western Tradition

In his Preface to the *Critique of Pure Reason*, Immanuel Kant (1724–1804) declares: "It always remains a scandal of philosophy and universal human reason that the existence of things outside us ... should have to be assumed merely on faith, and that if it occurs to anyone to doubt it, we should be unable to answer him with a satisfactory proof."[1] But, later, in *Being and Time*, Martin Heidegger (1889–1976) responds: "The 'scandal of philosophy' is not that this proof has yet to be given, but that such proofs are expected and attempted again and again."[2]

Twentieth-century existentialism owes much to Heidegger's "existential phenomenology," which rejects metaphysical speculation regarding what lies "outside" the mind in favor of a phenomenological approach to the question of meaning. Phenomenology invites us to set aside assumptions about what is objectively "real" and instead pay attention to the specific contours of our immediate existence. We will find, Heidegger says, not a world bifurcated into objective matter and subjective perceptions but rather an immersive totality already familiar to us—a meaningful world full of value-laden items and human-centered projects. In this sense, to be a "thing" at all is always to be a meaningful thing situated in a web of human relations. There are no "things" outside of this immersive experiential totality, just as there are no "selves" apart from the world of things— Heidegger dares us to search our *own* experience of reality and conclude otherwise.

The phenomenological turn in existentialism is widely influential, but, as we will see in what follows, Kant's "scandal of philosophy" keeps coming back.[3] We begin with a recent debate between contemporary philosophers Susan Wolf and Steven Cahn, which frames the question of meaning in life in precisely the scandalous manner that Heidegger resists. In investigating the roots of their debate, we not only gain insight into why this scandal arises again and again in the history of Western thought, but we also become better able to evaluate the theoretical and practical success of the answer to this scandal that phenomenologists such as Heidegger propose. As we will see by the end, the problem is not that phenomenological existentialism lacks theoretical clarity, but rather it lacks a repertoire of techniques by which its non-dualistic account of meaning-making can be enacted in daily life.

The Ins and Outs of Meaning in Life

In a formula that philosopher Susan Wolf has stated in multiple publications, "Meaning arises when subjective attraction meets objective attractiveness."[4] In other words, the conditions for a meaningful life require that I be personally fulfilled by activities that are objectively valuable or worthwhile. As Wolf explains, the first half of the equation speaks to the subjective dimension: "A person is actively engaged by something if she is gripped, excited, involved by it."[5] The second half gestures toward the objective:

> That a meaningful life must involve "projects of worth" will, I expect, be more controversial, for the phrase hints of a commitment to some sort of objective value …. What is clear to me is that there can be no sense to the idea of meaningful lives without a distinction between more and less worthwhile ways to spend one's time, where the test of worth is at least partly independent of a person's preferences or enjoyment.[6]

She admits that she herself has no philosophical theory to explain what might count as an objective value, but she nonetheless sees the objective component as necessary, unless we are willing to admit that devoting ourselves passionately to a trivial activity is "meaningful."

Several critics of Wolf have predictably retorted, "Why not?" Or, as Steven Cahn says: "Why not allow others to pursue their own ways of life without disparaging their choices and declaring their lives meaningless? If a person finds delights that bring no harm, such a discovery should not be denigrated but appreciated."[7] A meaningful life is, for Cahn, precisely a life that I find meaningful—i.e., a life that I find personally fulfilling, regardless of whether what I am doing is "really" trivial or not.

Many people, I would predict, will side with Cahn in this debate. Given that no one, Wolf included, has a satisfying definition of what counts as an objective value, then it seems that we should hesitate before judging that other people's life projects are not worthwhile. Nonetheless, Wolf's equation does provoke a compelling question: If meaning is *only* the subjective experience of personal fulfillment, and if we let go of the objective dimension altogether, then do we not concede to nihilism in the end? That is, if meaning lives and dies with humans, or other sentient beings, then a universe devoid of sentience is still a cold, dead, meaningless place. Cahn himself seems to admit this, when, at the end of his commentary on Wolf's thesis, he cites the book of Ecclesiastes: "Even if a man lives many years, let him enjoy himself in all of them, remembering how many the days of darkness are going to be."[8] Live meaningfully while you can, this quote suggests, because death will erase us all in the end.

The debate between Wolf and Cahn helps lay out several dilemmas that arise when questions of meaning are framed by an implicit (or explicit) understanding of subject–object dualism. If we agree with Wolf that some activities or projects are objectively meaningful, then not only we are tasked with deciding what counts as objective meaning, but we face larger epistemological issues of how we know anything "objectively" at all. Yet if we agree with Cahn that meaning is purely subjective, then we face not only the specter of nihilism but a wider range of metaphysical issues regarding the status of so-called subjective reality. The remainder of the chapter contextualizes the above claims in greater detail, surveying key episodes from the intellectual history of Western philosophy, from seventeenth-century empiricism to twentieth-century existentialism and phenomenology.

As we will see, Western philosophy is stuck in a loop, at least in terms of the subject–object dualism that underlies the Wolf–Cahn debate and seems to restrict existential inquiry more broadly. Again and again, the Western tradition returns to the troubling realization that we can describe our own internal experiences with some degree of certainty, but we are at a loss when asked to confirm whether the external world itself in any way resembles our impressions of it. Although neither Wolf nor Cahn wishes to entangle the question of meaning in the epistemological and metaphysical difficulties outlined below, nonetheless their debate is informed by these dilemmas and the subject–object dualism that generates them.

Dilemmas of Objectivity

One way to satisfy Wolf's requirement that meaning in life be grounded in objectivity would be to turn to religion. For example, if we believe that there is one true God who created us for a reason, then we may understand Wolf's formula as saying that meaning arises when I derive personal fulfillment from carrying out the worthwhile purpose that God intended. The value of this God-given purpose would be, as Wolf says above, "at least partly independent of a person's preferences or enjoyment."[9] This underscores a key feature of the subject–object divide as usually understood in Western discourses: whereas matters of personal taste are not debatable, questions of objective truth do have right and wrong answers. Ultimately, the foodie cannot fault the fast food junkie for liking what she likes, but the saint can indeed tell the sinner to go to hell.

Western philosophers have often aspired to this level of objective certainty in their investigations into the nature of truth and reality. For example, the great thirteenth-century Catholic theologian Thomas Aquinas (1225–74), building on everything he inherited from the ancient Greek philosopher Aristotle (384–322 BCE), states: "A judgment is said to be true when it conforms to the external reality."[10] This medieval insight likely still captures many people's everyday intuitions about what it means to make a claim that is true or false. Philosophers today would call it the "correspondence theory" of truth. It means, roughly, that when I declare something to be true, then what I say ought to reflect conditions in the real world—when I tell you that the flower is yellow, then the flower should "really" be yellow. If, to the contrary, the flower is not "really" yellow, then I am either lying or wrong.

The correspondence theory of truth quickly raises epistemological issues: How do I know what conditions are like in the external world? For example, where I see yellow, a honeybee sees ultraviolet. Which one of us is right? What color is the flower "really"? In the eighteenth century, Kant made the once-radical claim that what people can know is directly correlated to their mental and sensory capacities. In other words, what human eyes cannot see will remain outside the bounds of human experience, and likewise what human minds cannot conceive will be beyond the grasp of our knowledge. As this shows, the correspondence theory is strained if our perceptions of the external world are not reliable.

We will return to the consequences of Kant's philosophy later in this chapter. For now, I would like to emphasize the ethical and political issues at stake if we set Kant aside and appeal instead to what has been called "direct realism" or "naïve realism." This is the notion that, regardless of the honeybee, our minds generally do give us an accurate picture of conditions in the external world. The well-known analytic philosopher Simon Blackburn declares that some version of direct realism is "the natural view of people everywhere, and of philosophers when they are off-duty."[11] However, he continues, this view "remains naïve until it is buttressed by explanations of how experience may change while things do not, how illusion is possible, how colours and sounds can be regarded as properties of things independent of us, and so forth."[12] In other words, although we may puzzle for now over the question of whether a flower is yellow or ultraviolet, we should not let this sway us toward far-fetched philosophical theories—sensible people are realists.

Nonetheless, contemporary continental philosophy and critical theory do raise legitimate concerns about the underlying motives driving claims to objective truth. As some will argue, the so-called objective perspective does not give us direct access to the external world so much as it gives us insight into who is in power in specific social contexts. Friedrich Nietzsche's (1844–1900) comparison of truth claims to power grabs[13] influenced the constructivist theories of Michel Foucault as well as a range of critical studies in areas such as feminism, queer theory, and race theory. As theorist Nina Gregg writes: "The critique of science made by radical feminists finds that objectivity, when elevated to the status of sole criterion of truth, masks interests in its claim to neutrality, devalues people's experiences and perceptions of reality, constitutes an invitation to domination, and claims for science an authority which disguises power as truth."[14] We need only recall the pseudo-scientific appeals to biology used to define "race," rank people by skin color, and thereby justify the slave trade, in order to understand the real and bloody consequences of disguising power as truth.

To respond to this critique, contemporary science needs more advanced epistemological tools than naïve realism. One attractive feature of scientific truth claims is that they are *fallible*, that is, subject to revision in light of new evidence. Can an answer to the question of meaning in life arise from sophisticated and responsible scientific investigation? This is the premise of E. O. Wilson's 2014 book *The Meaning of Human Existence*, which aims to give an "ultimate" explanation of human purpose as this might be understood in the biological sciences:

> In biology, how-and-why explanations are routine and expressed as "proximate" and "ultimate" causation of living processes. An example of the proximate is this: we have two hands and ten fingers, with which we do thus and so. The ultimate explanation is why we have two hands and ten fingers to start with, and why are we prone with them to do thus and so and not something else. The proximate explanation recognizes that anatomy and emotions are hardwired to engage in certain activities. The ultimate explanation answers the question, why this particular hardwiring and not some other? To explain the human condition, thereby to give meaning to the human existence, requires both levels of explanation.[15]

He clarifies that his understanding of "meaning" in human existence does not refer to any pre-given (or God-given) purpose but rather to the level of self-awareness we have achieved thanks to our particular evolutionary path—our ability to do what we mean, as it were, and to mean what we do:

> A spider spinning its web intends, whether conscious of the outcome or not, to catch a fly. That is the meaning of the web. The human brain evolved under the same regimen as the spider's web. Every decision made by a human being has meaning in the first, intentional sense. But the capacity to decide, and how and why the capacity came into being, and the consequences that followed, are the broader, science-based meaning of human existence.[16]

Under these conditions, Wilson's ultimate explanation of the human condition is simple enough: "Humanity arose as an accident of evolution, a product of random mutation and natural selection."[17] Though we may wish otherwise, he says, "there is no evidence of an external grace shining down upon us, no demonstrable destiny or purpose assigned us, no second life vouchsafed us for the end of the present one."[18] But, in this, he finds existential significance: "We are, it seems, completely alone. And that in my opinion is a very good thing. It means we are completely free."[19] Given our freedom and our current level of scientific achievement, Wilson is optimistic: "Laid before us are new options scarcely dreamed of in earlier ages. They empower us to address with more confidence the greatest goal of all time, the unity of the human race."[20]

So, as it turns out, the human condition is a product of chance evolutionary processes, and human purpose lies in exerting meaningful control over our future. Although I am sympathetic to Wilson's agnostic, naturalistic worldview, I find his existential conclusions unsatisfying. When I raise the question of meaning in life, I am hoping for more than a declaration of human freedom against the unthinking forces of nature. Moreover, I do not share Wilson's strong rejection of religiosity or his confidence in dismissing all phenomena usually consigned to the category "supernatural." I am especially disturbed by his suggestion that the ultimate goal—which he defines, somewhat ominously, as "the unity of the human race"—requires the eradication of religious belief and religious believers. He draws an analogy to parasitic infestation: "Destructive inborn traits of social life can be viewed as a parallel of the physical presence of parasitic organisms, and the cultural diminishment of their impact as the lessening of a tolerable dogma load. One obvious example of the latter is blind faith in supernatural creation stories."[21] Of course, he does not suggest physically eradicating religious believers, but he does entertain a range of scenarios in which they might be gently re-educated through varieties of public outing:

> To examine each of the [creation] stories in detail objectively and to spell out their known historical origins would be a good start .... A second step, granted an unrealistic one, would be to ask the leaders of each religion and sect, assisted by theologians, to publicly defend the supernatural details of their faiths in competition with other faiths and aided by natural-cause and historical analysis.[22]

Again, the cautionary perspective of continental philosophy and critical theory seems appropriate here—we should be wary of disguising power as truth before insisting that religious leaders get into the public square and duke it out.

Nonetheless, Wilson is right to say that the situation becomes more complicated when we ground truth claims not in science but in the absolutism of religious certainty. As was asked earlier, suppose we believe in one true God who created us for a purpose, and suppose we further believe that all humans should live their lives in accordance with that purpose. Our neighbors might be understandably suspicious if we run for political office on that platform. The known dangers of claims to absolute truth likely undergird Susan Wolf's own hesitation over spelling out exactly what she means by "objective value."

Part of the dilemma here is that we are working with a limited understanding of religion, religiosity, and the so-called supernatural. In Wilson's book, it is clear that he thinks all religions are similar to Western monotheisms—that is, he criticizes their unscientific creation stories, their pretensions to absolute and universal truths, and their competitive attitudes toward each other. Outside the limited scope of the West, we find that very few religious traditions operate this way. Hence the material in the coming chapters will help us reframe notions of meaning in ways that do not require so-called objective certainty, whether religious or naively scientific. That said, by rejecting this understanding of objectivity, I do not thereby propose that we accept the competing thesis—that meaning is purely subjective. That option, as discussed next, is beset with its own problems.

Dilemmas of Subjectivity

Doubts over the feasibility of direct realism have driven many philosophical twists and turns in the Western tradition, with Cartesian solipsism being an extreme example. In the opening of his *Meditations on First Philosophy*, René Descartes (1596–1650) despairs over the possibility that he is trapped in his own mind, that his so-called perceptions of the external world are merely subjective hallucinations or dreams. Can he know anything at all about the world outside of his own subjective experience? At this point, most philosophers would likely answer that he at least can know that certain logical and mathematical relations are true. But Descartes manages to doubt even these. An omnipotent being, he speculates, could cause him to be deceived about seemingly transparent truths, such as the notion that two added to three equals five, or that a square has four sides.[23] Although he later backs away from the claim that God could suspend the rules of logic,[24] Descartes nonetheless provides the upper limit on subjectivism: a single disembodied consciousness who is, for all it knows, alone in a void.

A less extreme case would be the subjective idealism of George Berkeley (1685–1753). Other thinkers in Berkeley's time, such as the empiricists Thomas Hobbes (1588–1679) and John Locke (1632–1704), took an agnostic approach to the question of mind-independent reality. Knowledge, they argued, is built up from basic sensory data: we experience sensations; we analyze, categorize, and reflect on these experiences; and eventually we manage to attain high levels of abstract, conceptual thought. Unlike Descartes, neither Hobbes nor Locke worries that the sensations are figments of our minds, but still they refrain from speculating about what external objects are, when unperceived by us—"things without us," as Hobbes says, are likely out there, but we can only know them as they appear when filtered through our subjective sense experiences.[25]

Berkeley, by contrast, pushes this thesis a step further. It is superfluous, he says, to continue believing in the existence of objects external to the mind, when they remain completely unperceivable to us; better to go ahead and admit that the nature of reality itself *is* subjective experience. In other words, everything that exists is either a mind or the experience of a mind, meaning that all so-called material reality is actually a mental phenomenon. Given that reality as a whole seems to exceed our individual human experiences of it, Berkeley completes his theory by concluding that the vastness of existence is contained in the mind of God.[26] From God's ultimate perspective, there is no such thing as mind-independent reality, but from a single person's limited perspective, many mental objects are indeed outside of any one individual's purview.

The role played by God in Berkeley's theory helps to avoid a radical skepticism in which people would have no grounds for believing that their experiences conform to anything "real" at all. This possibility does not seem to bother Berkeley's successor David Hume (1711–76), who accepts much of Berkeley's skepticism but eliminates the reference to God. What, asks Hume, is causality? Nothing, he says, but a habit of the mind, grounded in our perception that event B always follows event A, as far as we can tell.[27] What is the "self"? Nothing but a string of past and present experiences linked together in our awareness, to which we impute a sense of continuity. "For my part," writes Hume, "when I enter most intimately into what I call *myself*, I always stumble on some particular perception or other, of heat or cold, light or shade, love or hatred, pain or pleasure. I never can catch *myself* at any time without a perception, and never can observe anything but the perception."[28] Although Hume, like Hobbes, Locke, and Berkeley, does not entertain Cartesian solipsism, his skepticism is, in many ways, just as extreme. Descartes can at least tell us, "I think, therefore I am," but Hume will only go so far as to say that some sort of thinking is, indeed, happening.

Entering into these debates over idealism, realism, empiricism, and rationalism, Kant describes his philosophy as radical (a "Copernican" revolution[29]), but in many ways he retreads territory already covered by his predecessors. For one, Kant accepts the basic distinction between inner experiences and external objects, or, in his terms, between noumena (things as they are unperceived by us) and phenomena (things as they appear to us via our sensations and perceptions). Also, Kant accepts Hume's claim that some aspects of experience, such as causality, are not "out there" as real qualities of objects or relations between objects but rather are features of human awareness.

Kant goes further, however, in showing that such aspects are not merely contingent features of our awareness but instead are the conditions for any coherent experience at all—thereby setting the stage for future phenomenology. His basic theoretical account of human knowledge has two parts: sensation, followed by understanding.[30] Sensation refers to our contact with external objects via our senses. In order for an object to be sensed by us, it must appear in space and time—that is, it must have some perceptible dimension, and it must last for at least a nanosecond, or else it would escape our attention altogether. Hence, Kant says, space and time are not features of objective reality but are the very conditions for sensation. In turn, when sensations are "understood," they are processed by the conceptual mind according to Kant's fundamental categories of quantity, quality, relation, and modality. Again, these are not features of the external world but are the conditions that make conceptual understanding and higher-order rational thought possible.

So, unlike the British empiricists before him, Kant does not think that all knowledge of abstract concepts is built up from sense experience, for the categories of conceptual understanding themselves are part of the pre-given apparatus of the human mind. But, unlike continental rationalists such as Descartes, neither does Kant think that the human mind achieves knowledge via its innate ideas alone—the categories cannot give us knowledge without the rich content of sense experience. This is summed up in Kant's famous formula: "Thoughts without content are empty, intuitions without concepts are blind."[31]

All in all, perhaps the most important consequence for later philosophical thought, both continental and analytic, is Kant's strong critique of metaphysical speculation—if the noumenal aspects of simple physical objects are outside the bounds of human experience, then so too are ultimate metaphysical realities, whatever those might be. For Kant, the answers to such metaphysical questions can safely be set aside or relegated to the realm of religion.

Returning to the debate over meaning between Wolf and Cahn, we see that their disagreement rehashes familiar idealist and realist positions: Either meaning is objective and hence exists independently of us, or it is a subjective feature of mental experience and nothing more. Cahn's rejection of a realist account of meaning is in line with the general turn against metaphysical speculation going back to at least seventeenth-century Europe. The stance against realism—especially as it pertains to abstract concepts such as meaning, causality, or goodness—appeals to our intuitive sense that we have direct access to our own interior lives in ways that we do not have access to conditions in the external world. Cahn's position contrasts with a contemporary realist such as E. O. Wilson, who says that meaning is not merely a subjective human experience but rather a real feature of our evolutionary biology, which itself attests to natural processes that exist independently of us. It also contrasts with a Western religious perspective, which might say that meaning is provided through God's design. However, as we saw, both realist positions warrant caution, given that claims to objective certainty are associated with problems of determinism, absolutism, and even authoritarianism. So, faced with a variety of unsatisfying options, we should question the premise that generates them—i.e., subject–object dualism. This is the approach taken by Nietzsche and many of the existential philosophers that followed him, and the extent to which any of these are successful in overcoming this entrenched dualism is the topic of the rest of this chapter.

Nietzsche and Value-Creation

Before Nietzsche, both Hume and Kant also offered critiques of Cartesian dualism, especially the idea that the self is a sort of metaphysical substance possessing certain properties, such as thought, as expressed in Descartes's formulation that the self is a "thinking thing" (*res cogitans*) as opposed to material substance, which is an "extended thing" (*res extensa*). Hume, as we saw, rejects this claim that the self is a metaphysical entity, arguing instead that what we believe to be the self is nothing more than a series of experiences connected in memory. Kant suspends the question, effectively saying that, even if Hume is right, our self-awareness of having such memories relies on the "transcendental unity of apperception," or "transcendental subject,"[32] which, like other Kantian conditions for experience, cannot itself become an object *of* experience. In both cases, a certain version of subject–object duality is avoided—there can be no such dualism when there is no subject in the first place.

Only with Nietzsche do we find a sustained investigation into the existential implications of this critique of subjectivity for the human condition. In *Thus Spoke Zarathustra*, Nietzsche's mountain hermit declares: "'Body am I and soul'—thus talks the child. And why should one not talk like children? But the awakened one, the one who knows, says: Body am I through and through, and nothing besides; and soul is merely a word for something about the body."[33] The metaphysical subject, Nietzsche says, is an outdated fiction, and one that we should seek to overcome. It is our "most recent creation,"[34] but other ways of being are possible. Through Zarathustra, Nietzsche expresses unabated optimism over the constructive force of this philosophy:

> The human being first put values into things, in order to preserve itself—it created a meaning for things, a human's meaning! Therefore it calls itself 'human'—that is, the evaluator.
>
> Evaluating is creating: hear this, you creators! Evaluating is itself the treasure and jewel of all valued things.
>
> Through evaluating alone is there value: and without evaluating the kernel of existence would be hollow. Hear this, you creators!
>
> Change of values—that means change of creators. Whoever must be a creator always annihilates.[35]

It is a radical vision: new human beings, who appear after the overcoming of the metaphysical subject, will be the creators of new values, new human conditions, and new worlds.

This creation is fueled by the "will to power," which Nietzsche contrasts with a "will to truth." Were we to ask about what is *really* meaningful, and were we to assume that some answer might be discovered "out there" already pre-given in the world, then we would express the will to truth. We would seek objective certainty. But, Nietzsche says, the will to truth is another outdated fiction. Hence, along with the overcoming of the metaphysical subject, there is a concurrent breakdown on the other side of subject-object dualism—there is no metaphysically robust objective reality to which the will to power must conform. As the comparative philosopher Graham

Parkes says, in one of his many cross-cultural engagements with Nietzsche, "When this belief in the I-substance is undermined, the concept of the 'thing' is correspondingly weakened, and what comes to the fore as substance recedes is (as in Buddhism) *relationships*."[36]

Taking seriously Parkes's reference to Buddhism, we can see that the will to power does indeed mark a radical break with subject–object duality: such a will goes beyond mere personal intentions, and the values it creates are not simply imposed upon a preexisting objective world. But, how do we accomplish the feat of this non-egoic willing? How do we attain this power? Even a full survey of all of Nietzsche's writings will not yield a conclusive answer. My guiding thesis in the book as a whole is that existential philosophy repeatedly sees the reemergence of subject–object dualism and all of the attendant problems, because it lacks a clearly articulated plan of practice for enacting its own non-dualistic theoretical insights.

As a case in point, in contemporary mainstream (i.e., non-cross-cultural) philosophy, Nietzsche's notion of value-creation is routinely parsed according to subject–object dualism. In a 2018 article, Harold Langsam summarizes this succinctly: "Let us say that values that are created by human subjects are *subjective* values. Nietzsche is a *subjectivist* in that he holds that the only values that exist are subjective values. A value is *objective* if it is not subjective; in denying that anything has value 'in itself', Nietzsche is denying that there are any objective values."[37] This, says Langsam, raises the question of whether we must essentially trick ourselves into believing in the objective reality of the values we concoct. In other words, as with our earlier discussion of the nihilism lurking in Cahn's account of subjective meaning, it seems that a subjectivist must ultimately admit that nothing is "really" meaningful. Some contemporary philosophers try to work with this, describing Nietzsche's understanding of values as a "fictionalist" or "error theorist" approach. As Nadeem Hussain says, in an article on Nietzsche and fictionalism, "There is a widespread, popular view—and one I will basically endorse—that Nietzsche is, in one sense of the word, a nihilist."[38] Hussain's intriguing but somewhat unsatisfying conclusion is that "Nietzsche's free spirits engage in a simulacrum of valuing by regarding things as valuable in themselves while knowing that they are not."[39] On this model, recalling Wolf's formula for meaningfulness, living a meaningful life will inevitably require a degree of earnest play-acting.

Other scholars have tried to avoid this outcome. Andrew Huddleston lays out enough textual evidence to show that it is at least not inconsistent with Nietzsche's writings to say that some values may be "accurate to evaluative facts (if not necessarily to *mind-independent* evaluative facts) and thereby to have genuine value," where "genuine" is defined not as metaphysically real but as corresponding to some actual state of affairs, even if this state of affairs is not mind-independent.[40] In other words, the "real" state of affairs to which values correspond are subjective states, that is, the ways that people really do feel about what is valuable. Alex Silk draws a similar conclusion, when he refers to Nietzsche as a metaethical constructivist: "Metaethical constructivists accept that normative properties are attitude-dependent .... Normative facts, on this view, are nothing 'over and above' facts about agents' evaluative attitudes."[41] Elsewhere, Maudemarie Clark and David Dudrick build on this reasoning when they say that "objectivity" for Nietzsche involves the ability to inhabit multiple subjective perspectives, to see things from others' perspectives, and not be limited by one's own personal attitudes and inclinations. Creators of values cultivate precisely this ability: "He can create values in good intellectual conscience only because, having inhabited many different evaluative perspectives, he deems himself to have achieved a very serious degree of objectivity."[42]

Peter Poellner refers to this sense of objectivity as "phenomenally objective," where "phenomenal" is used in the Kantian sense to refer to reality as it is perceived by humans. So, like Huddleston, Silk, Clark, and Dudrick, Poellner sets the issue of metaphysical realism aside: "The question whether values are not only phenomenally objective, but real in a metaphysical sense, is of practical relevance only if we are committed to what Nietzsche calls the 'will to truth'. For those not subject to this 'kernel' of the 'ascetic ideal' (GM III. 27), the metaphysical status of value can rationally be a matter of indifference."[43] In general, twentieth-century phenomenology accepts this approach—better, they say, to restrict philosophical investigation to phenomenal experience and leave metaphysical reality alone. Following Nietzsche, the first metaphysical item taken off the table is the subject itself. By suspending the question of the subject, phenomenology aims instead to focus on the immediacy of lived experience. Heidegger's famous phrase "being-in-the-world" is meant to signal precisely the overcoming of subject–object duality and a turn toward the immersive totality of phenomenal existence.[44] As such, phenomenology seems to be the best option so far for taking up Nietzsche's projects of value-creation and existential self-determination, as perhaps exemplified in Simone de Beauvoir's 1947 work *Ethics of Ambiguity*.

Beauvoir and the Existential Condition

Human consciousness, for Beauvoir, both seeks and creates meaning, but it operates under certain constraints of the human condition: (1) it is born into a world where certain values (often oppressive values) are already deeply entrenched, and (2) it is limited by a number of perpetual uncertainties, including the unknowability of the future, the imminence of death, and the apparent nonexistence of any absolute truth or God-given purpose in life. Because of such uncertainties, human meaning is always in part ambiguous; yet precisely because meaning is not predetermined, we are free to create: "Regardless of the staggering dimensions of the world about us, the density of our ignorance, the risks of catastrophes to come, and our individual weakness within the immense collectivity, the fact remains that we are absolutely free today if we choose to will our existence in its finiteness, a finiteness which is open on the infinite."[45]

Related to these notions of ambiguity and freedom, Beauvoir's work engages a number of terms that have become canonical within Western existentialism, including facticity, absurdity, and anxiety. *Facticity* refers to the bare facts of existence as we encounter them, not as conditions of our own choosing but often as obstacles to our will: "Man does not create the world. He succeeds in disclosing it only through the resistance which the world opposes to him. The will is defined only by raising obstacles, and by the contingency of facticity certain obstacles let themselves be conquered, and others do not."[46] The bare facts of existence often appear to us as *absurd*, or without reason. Why these facts, and not others? Why these human conditions, as opposed to other ways of being? Why are we living the lives that we are living, when nothing is meaningful in the end? The absurdity of the human condition can cause us *anxiety*, especially in the face of the unknown future. But, as Beauvoir says, "The notion of ambiguity must not be confused with that of absurdity. To declare that existence is absurd is to deny that it can ever be given a meaning; to say that it is ambiguous is to assert that its meaning is never fixed."[47]

The capacity for authentic meaning-making hinges on Beauvoir's understanding of the will, which echoes Nietzsche's earlier use of this term. As she says in the quote above, we are free "if we choose to will our existence in its finiteness."[48] By this, she means that we not only accept the human condition in which we find ourselves but that we enthusiastically embrace it as the ground upon which we build better versions of ourselves and our world: "It is a matter of reconquering freedom on the contingent facticity of existence, that is, of taking the given, which, at the start, *is there* without any reason, as something willed by man. A conquest of this kind is never finished; the contingency remains."[49] The moral sensibility that guides us, in our freedom, is a resistance to any human-constructed way of life that oppresses others, that is, that denies others their own existential freedom and creativity. Hence, Beauvoir concludes, her ethics is not individualistic in the sense of being driven by the whims of a solitary ego, but nonetheless it does accord "to the individual an absolute value and … recognizes in him alone the power of laying the foundations of his own existence."[50]

Here, we see the familiar subject–object dynamic at play, in the form of the subjective momentum that drives meaning-making. As such, certain familiar dilemmas emerge, similar to the questions posed above to Nietzsche as whether he might be a "fictionalist," an "error-theorist," or a "nihilist." As Beauvoir herself asks: "Yet isn't this battle without victory pure gullibility? … isn't it simply a matter of organizing among men a complicity which allows them to substitute a game of illusions for the given world?"[51] She answers: We cannot criticize human-made meaning as an "illusion" unless we secretly uphold some notion of absolute truth or metaphysical reality against which human constructions can be judged. Logically, this is convincing, even compelling—the illusion–reality binary is indeed indebted to the very metaphysics that existentialism and phenomenology reject. But, ultimately, it returns us to the position of Steven Cahn, and his resigned acceptance of the eventual futility of all human endeavors. Even if Beauvoir's emphasis on the transience of human meaning is well-placed (and, in the next chapter on Buddhism, we will see that it is), her account of the individual will that makes such meaning possible leaves us with the same question as did Nietzsche's declarations on value-creation: How do we *do* any of this?

Dilemmas of Phenomenology

Note, at this point, none of the thinkers we have discussed give a robust refutation of Cartesian solipsism; they all seem to assume that reasonable people can set aside their concerns about that extreme and highly unlikely scenario. Perhaps this helps explain the return of solipsism in the innovative critique of phenomenology put forward by Quentin Meillassoux in *After Finitude*, a text which has come to be associated with the loosely related philosophical movements of speculative realism, new materialism, and object-oriented ontology. In short, as his argument goes, since at least the time of Kant's distinction between noumena and phenomena, phenomenologists have accepted the thesis that our understanding of reality is correlated with our capacity for understanding, that is, with our own perceptual and cognitive abilities and limitations. Meillassoux makes the even stronger claim that philosophers correlate being, or existence itself, with the experience of being, which produces what he says "could be called a 'species solipsism', or a 'solipsism of the community', since it ratifies the impossibility of thinking any reality that would be anterior or posterior to the community of thinking beings."[52] As a result, we lose access to the "great outdoors,"[53] which is to say, we lose the ability to make any sense of mind-independent reality. Meillassoux calls for renewed realism—a "speculative realism"—that can once again investigate the great outdoors, without returning to the assumptions of a naïve realism in which we simply have unimpeded access to what we know and perceive.

Of course, many phenomenologists might resist this critique, pointing out that even Kant assumed that the sources of our sensations are located in mind-independent reality. But Meillassoux is quite right to say that post-Kantian philosophy at large has renounced the task of investigating that reality—it makes no sense, for either Kant or the phenomenologists, to turn our philosophical attention to the noumenal world. By rejecting the metaphysical subject, phenomenologists effectively reduce the issue of what lies "outside" the mind to a poorly phrased question. And yet, returning to Heidegger's comment with which this chapter opened, the scandal of philosophy always seems to draw us back in.

In his excellent 2014 book *The End of Phenomenology: Metaphysics and the New Realism*, Tom Sparrow supplies convincing evidence that phenomenology never does get beyond "the idealist/realist duality."[54] As he argues, phenomenology swings variously between positions of idealism and antirealism, generally adopting an agnostic approach to questions of metaphysics and mind-independent reality while trying to avoid the charge that it turns into classic subjective idealism in the end. As Sparrow says, "Take Sartre, for example. He consistently describes the self, others, and objects as 'concrete' presences so that readers are reminded that he is talking about things that are right there in front of us, everyday real things, even if it sounds like he is repeating familiar idealist analyses."[55] Taking us back to the existential dimensions of our discussion, Sparrow comments that this rhetoric of concreteness "is the hallmark of phenomenology's existential turn."[56] He explains: "It is made up of a constellation of terms intended to denote immediacy and corporeality, including 'embodiment,' 'thrownness,' 'facticity,' 'existential,' 'immanence,' 'lifeworld,' 'concrete,' 'pregiven,' 'praxis,' and the famous slogan 'Back to the things themselves!'"[57]

Despite its rhetoric, Sparrow doubts that phenomenology achieves its stated goals. Not unlike the way Berkeley encouraged his empiricist colleagues to concede the obvious, Sparrow suggests in his conclusion that phenomenologists consider a return "to phenomenology's idealist roots. Not the transcendental idealism of Kant, however, or the neo-Kantianism to which Husserl and Heidegger were responding, but the absolute idealism of Hegel, the original phenomenology."[58] Via this route, Sparrow says, perhaps phenomenology can have "a speculative future."[59] In other words, the spiritual monism of G. W. F. Hegel (1770–1831) can play a role for phenomenology similar to the role that the mind of God played for Berkeley, helping to guard against certain skeptical and solipsistic tendencies.

At this point, however, before we all become Hegelians, I would like to return to my earlier remark that philosophy is stuck in a loop—we are at an impasse defined by a long intellectual history of debates that never do address the basic anxiety of Cartesian solipsism, which is to say, we find ourselves again and again staring down the borders of subjective experience, unable to see what lies beyond. Perhaps our problem is not that we lack theoretical resources for articulating a non-dualistic existential philosophy, but we lack practices for enacting our theories in the long term. Without practical techniques to effectively re-*habituate* existentialism, it seems that the scandal of philosophy will inevitably recur.

Hence, in what follows, we exit the confines of the Western tradition and revisit our existential questions within intellectual histories not defined by the dualities of subject and object or idealism and realism. Over the course of the next three chapters, we engage Asian discourses that not only provide robust theoretical accounts of the immersive totality of experience central to phenomenology, but that also leave ample room for speculative existential investigation and, moreover, teach specific techniques for meaningfully transforming the lives that we live. These traditions offer, in short, lessons in the *practice* of making meaning.

2

The Creation of New Values, Part I: Karmic Transformations

I cannot exist entirely except when somehow I go beyond the stage of action. Otherwise I'm a soldier, a professional, a man of learning, not a "total human being." The fragmentary state of humanity is basically the same as the choice of an object. When you limit your desires to possessing political power, for instance, you act and know what you have to do .... right from the start, you insert your existence advantageously into time. Each of your moments becomes useful. With each moment, the possibility is given you to advance to some chosen goal, and your time becomes a march toward that goal—what's normally called living.

—Georges Bataille[1]

Being attached to the fragments of our own thoughts, we have lost the universal "I" and mistake the "I" that is as small as a particle of dust for the great "I." ... Once an individual is capable of uniting her own thoughts and their opposites and her actions are in accord with the unity of opposites, she is fully in charge of a change in her body .... Anyone desirous of achieving such a state in this life should join a monastery, or, if that is not possible, one should practice concentration to attain the total power of mind. Only then will that person be free in her own actions.

—Kim Iryŏp[2]

One key insight of existential philosophy is that meaning and value are only comprehensible within a given context: a word is meaningful within a certain language, paper bills are valuable within a certain system of finance, or (to borrow Heidegger's famous example[3]) tools are useful only in light of certain tasks. We have already seen several attempts to locate the meaning of human life within an all-encompassing context, such as God's design or scientific empiricism. In contrast, Georges Bataille—Nietzsche's self-proclaimed soulmate—provides a stark rejection of any such attempt to render meaning intelligible relative to the bounds of a specific narrative. In this chapter, we expand on Bataille's brief writings on the Buddhist tradition to explore the radical potential of trans-egoic value creation.

Our goal is to understand the provocative claims of the twentieth-century Buddhist nun Kim Iryŏp that (1) the mind of a meditator generates a potent energy that reaches beyond the bounds of the body, (2) this energy is capable of transforming our shared existential conditions, and hence (3) enlightened beings are creators of new values. Contextualizing Iryŏp's claims requires a study of Buddhist teachings on karma as well as practices related to generating karmic merit and transferring it between beings. To bring out the existential dimensions of this karmic economy, we begin below with a look at Bataille's own engagement with Buddhism in his two-part epic on economics, *The Accursed Share*.

Bataille's Existential Economics

In *The Accursed Share*, Bataille criticizes the budgeting of human life as determined by the instrumental value of our actions. Only within the limited context of what he calls a "restricted economy" can we make sense of human projects "in terms of particular operations with limited ends."[4] Such a restricted system is merely a façade projected upon our true existential situation, in which life in general is neither directed toward nor constrained by any particular ends at all:

> Economic science merely generalizes the isolated situation; it restricts its object to operations carried out with a view to a limited end, that of economic man. It does not take into consideration a play of energy that no particular end limits: the play of *living matter in general* .... On the surface of the globe for *living matter in general* energy is always in excess; the question is always posed in terms of extravagance. The choice is limited to how the wealth is to be squandered.[5]

By this, Bataille does not mean that energy is simply limitless or that planets are impervious to total catastrophe. Rather, he means that to *be* at all—the fact that there is something rather than nothing—is already entirely gratuitous, in the sense of being ungrounded as well as free. All limited systems that we project over this existential freedom are doomed to break down eventually. Bataille calls this the principle of "general economy."

On the one hand, this principle casts doubt on the viability of existential projects from that of E. O. Wilson to Simone de Beauvoir, by challenging the optimism that we could ever construct for ourselves a "better world," a better limited system, that is sustainable in the long term. On the other hand, Bataille does speculate that we could assume creative control over these processes of construction and destruction, if we were able to face up to our existential situation: "Our ignorance only has this incontestable effect: It causes us to undergo what we could bring about in our own way, if we understood."[6] A true creator—a bringer of new values in Nietzsche's sense—could exert some authorship over the inevitable breakdown of limited systems of meaning and usher in new worlds, perhaps avoiding what Bataille describes as the "catastrophic destructions" that usually overwhelm us.[7]

In an effort to investigate this possibility, Bataille presents a series of case studies to illustrate a variety of restricted systems and analyze their eventual demise. He points to practices of human sacrifice and potlatch as examples of economic systems premised on the extravagant squandering of resources, and he contrasts these with our contemporary capitalist system, which he considers an example of extravagant accumulation. All of these cases are meant to illustrate his central claim that limited economic systems are doomed not by scarcity or lack but by the extravagance—the gratuitousness—of being itself, often resulting in growth to the point of self-destruction. In many cases, rather than face the breakdown of the context in which their lives have meaning, people will cling to the old system at all costs, until it destroys them.

Another of Bataille's case studies is the monastic system in place in Tibet prior to annexation under Maoist forces in the 1950s. Monasticism, says Bataille, is a much less bloody strategy for thriving in relation to the principle of general economy: "Thus in the midst of a richer and well-armed world, the poor country in its closed container must give the problem of surplus a solution that checks its explosive violence within: an internal construction so perfect ... so unconducive to accumulation, that one cannot envisage the least growth of the system."[8] He goes on to explain: "The celibacy of the monks even presented a threat of depopulation .... The revenue of the monasteries ensured the consumption of resources, supporting a mass of sterile consumers .... Lamaism is the opposite of the other systems: it alone avoids activity, which is always directed toward acquisition and growth."[9]

Too bad for Bataille that he did not dig deeper into Buddhist practice, where he would have seen that Buddhist monks, too, are in the business of extravagant accumulation. Within the Buddhist karmic economy, karmic merit exhibits the odd behavior of increasing even when it is used or given away; or, in other words, this economy is premised not on scarcity or lack but on the rampant production of *new value*. Given Buddhism's philosophical commitments, it comes much closer than Bataille realizes to articulating what he seeks—a proposal for thriving in the midst of the inevitable breakdown of all limited systems of meaning. In what follows, we travel from the earliest recorded teachings of Śākyamuni Buddha to the existential philosophy of a twentieth-century Korean nun, to examine the proliferation of karmic merit as a mode of existential meaning-making.

Buddhism and the Karmic Economy

Buddhist cosmology can be thought of as a multiverse of numerous world-systems, most containing multiple planes of existence, including various hellish and heavenly realms. Rebirth on a different plane, or into a different world system altogether, is governed by a vast karmic calculus. In simplest terms, *karma* is the relation of cause and effect that links present states of existence to future ones. Whereas ordinary people will be propelled by karmic forces into renewed existence after death, a buddha, or awakened being, has attained liberation from those cycles of rebirth governed by karmic relations.

Insight into the nature and workings of karma constitute the core of Buddhist doctrine, or *dharma*. In its simplest formulation, dharma proclaims the Four Noble Truths, regarding the existence of suffering, the cause of suffering, the overcoming of suffering, and the path to liberation. The first and second Noble Truths speak to the interrelatedness of suffering (Sk. *duḥka*), impermanence (*anitya*), and non-substantiality or "no-self" (*anātman*), which are often referred to as the "Three Marks," or the three features that characterize all of existence. Together these express that all existing forms are temporary, including our "selves," and our resistance to the inevitable transience of life is the root cause of our suffering. Accordingly, the third Noble Truth teaches that suffering can be overcome if we can relinquish this resistance. The way to relinquish the desires and attachments that cause our suffering is named in the last Noble Truth as the Eightfold Path, a practical agenda for banishing ignorance, developing wisdom, living in accord with our ever-changing conditions, and cultivating the powers of mind (awareness and concentration) that allow for the sustained liberatory practice of a buddha.

The Four Noble Truths operate according to the karmic logic of cause and effect—suffering has a cause, and hence suffering can be undone when the cause is addressed. But this formulation should not be taken to oversimplify the complexity of the human condition. Karmic causality is rarely, if ever, a matter of a single agent, a single action, and a single result. To the contrary, the temporary self is the product of karmic conditions as much as it is an agent of future consequences; likewise, it can be the victim of conditions it did not create as much as it can contribute to conditions that affect others. All living beings are caught up in a network of interrelated and overlapping karmic relations, where actions arise from multiple causes, and consequences are amplified or mediated depending on the situation. As a result, undoing the karmic bonds that keep a single person tied to conditions of suffering is a nearly superhuman feat.

Yet, as we learn in the Pāli canon, a collection of the earliest known Buddhist writings, Śākyamuni Buddha began life here on earth as the human prince Siddhartha and attained nirvāṇa after several years of ascetic practice. That said, these few years are only the tip of an iceberg—a chain of karmic causes, extending back across numerous past lives, all contribute to the Buddha's rebirth as a prince in the Śākya clan, his disposition toward asceticism, and his eventual attainment of nirvāṇa. Despite some Buddhist modernist movements, which tend to downplay the seemingly supernormal aspects of the Pāli canon, the notion of multiple rebirths is central to the specific karmic machinery that underlies the nature and cause of suffering—i.e., *pratītyasamutpāda,* or "dependent origination." Upon his enlightenment, Śākyamuni Buddha declares his insight into the functioning of this karmic framework and comments that the details of his realization will certainly be difficult for others to grasp.[10]

According to the doctrine of dependent origination, the causal chains that bind us to "this whole mass of suffering" are mutually interdependent, but they are often delineated in a series of twelve steps, beginning with ignorance:

> Dependent on ignorance, there are dispositions to action; dependent on dispositions to action, there is consciousness; dependent on consciousness, there is psycho-physicality; dependent on psycho-physicality, there are the six bases of sense; dependent on the six bases of sense, there is contact; dependent on contact, there is feeling; dependent on feeling, there is craving; dependent on craving, there is attachment; dependent on attachment, there is becoming; dependent on becoming, there is birth; dependent on birth, there is aging-and-death, sorrow, lamentation, pain, despair, and distress. Thus there is the arising of this whole mass of suffering.[11]

Although all the steps are mutually reinforcing, the interlocking system seems to pivot at the point of consciousness and psycho-physicality, and several times in the Pāli literature the Buddha affirms their interdependence: "Thus, dependent on psycho-physicality, there is consciousness, and dependent on consciousness, there is psycho-physicality."[12] As this indicates, birth is but one instance in a series of events that repeat over and over again until the bonds of cause-and-effect are interrupted at some point along the chain. Usually, this begins by undoing our ignorance through a correct understanding of the Four Noble Truths.

Commenting on the specific role of rebirth in the Buddhist karmic framework, Thanissaro Bhikkhu writes:

> Only because he saw that birth was a repeated process did he probe into the causes of birth and trace them through the factors that he later taught in his description of dependent co-arising. In other words, if the Buddha hadn't assumed rebirth, he never would have discovered or taught the central tenets of his teaching: the four noble truths and dependent co-arising .... And as we will see, the Buddha discovered that the processes leading to suffering are self-sustaining, meaning that unless they are deliberately starved they will continue repeating indefinitely. In this way, not only birth, but also every factor in dependent co-arising is prefixed with an implicit "re-", from re-ignorance to re-death.[13]

What does it mean to "starve" the processes that sustain the cycles of birth, death, and rebirth? Answering this question requires an understanding of the institutional structures of Buddhism through which all beings participate in the co-creation of various world-systems.

Good Karma, Bad Karma, and No Karma

A key teaching of Buddhism is that all self-motivated actions produce karma, and *all* karma feeds the cycle of rebirth—in other words, even the fruits of our good deeds contribute to our continued suffering. In general, in the karmic economy, good deeds produce positive karma, or merit (*puṇya*), which leads to a better rebirth, where "better" is understood specifically to mean conditions more favorable to the attainment of enlightenment. In other words, a good rebirth might be in a location where the dharma is taught, in a family with the means to support an aspiring Buddhist, in a society with the monastic institutions where sustained Buddhist practice can be carried out, and so forth. A good rebirth might even mean being reborn in a heavenly realm as a god-like deva, who is not subject to physical pain. However, it is important to keep in mind that, in Buddhist analysis, even the devas in the heavens are nonetheless suffering. They are attached to their happiness, such that they are unmotivated to hear the dharma, and so they undoubtedly do not gain the right understanding of the Four Noble Truths that leads to liberation from the cycles of birth, death, and rebirth.

This last point illustrates the distinction in Buddhism between happiness and true liberation, which relates to differences often seen in the practices of laypeople as compared to the practices of monastics. Whereas many lay-practitioners aim to gain karmic merit for the sake of a good rebirth, or even worldly benefit in the present, the goal of monastic practice is to avoid the production of further karma altogether, whether positive or negative, for the sake of true liberation. To return to Thanissaro Bhikkhu's language, the monastic practitioner wants to "starve" the karmic energy that would otherwise feed the mutually reinforcing relations of cause-and-effect that bind ignorance to suffering.

And, finally, this reveals a central tension, in that monastic practice itself generates an enormous amount of merit. This would seem, at first glance, to set up monks and nuns for inevitable failure—they seek to starve their karmic output but produce untold quantities of karmic merit as a result. The trick, as it were, requires monastic practitioners to perform their practices without attachment to the fruits of their labor; or, in other words, to practice from the position of selflessness. By practicing with the right understanding of suffering, impermanence, and no-self, monastics break the chain of cause-and-effect that fuels continued rebirth. Moreover, laypeople themselves are able to partake in this liberatory activity when they support monks and nuns through monetary donations—donating to the monastery has the twofold benefit of generating karmic merit for the donor while at the same time linking the donor to the larger Buddhist project of escaping the bonds of karma altogether. It is absolutely a case of having the cake and eating it, too.

We can now see the full spectrum of the karmic economy: at one end, we have ordinary human beings, hindered by their ignorance, producing various amounts of good and bad karma leading to continuous rebirth under conditions of suffering. At the other end, we have a fully liberated buddha who can declare, as did Śākyamuni upon the moment of his enlightenment, "My liberation is unshakable. This is the last birth. There is now no rebirth."[14] In the Pāli canon, the fate of a fully awakened being upon death is left unanswered, but it is strongly implied to be complete extinguishment. Or, to be more precise, it is beyond even what might be described as "complete extinguishment," since the "self" who would be extinguished is already nonexistent, given the buddha's attainment of utter selflessness. As one passage elaborates, we cannot say that a buddha "exists after death," or "does not exist after death," or "both exists and does not exist after death," or "neither exists nor does not exist after death."[15]

As this suggests, for the average practitioner, whether lay or monastic, complete buddhahood is a distant (and possibly unappealing) goal. Between the two extremes of ignorant beings and liberated buddhas, there lay a range of interesting and surprising prospects for laypeople, monks, and nuns made possible by the unique features of karmic production and exchange.

Karma and the Extravagance of Compassion

In the earliest Buddhist sources, liberation is only possible through sustained meditative practice, which carries the practitioner through various stages of attainment, sometimes presented as levels of mental concentration but sometimes suggested to be different planes of spiritual existence.[16] Advancing through these stages is thought to take multiple lifetimes. Monastics are precisely those humans who have entered a monastery for the sake of beginning this journey. In contrast, laypeople have familial, social, and professional responsibilities that prevent them from taking the monastic route. However, as indicated above, interactions between laypeople and monastics are linked via a vast economic network, bound together by systems of monetary and karmic exchange, which allows lay-practitioners to partake in the liberatory activities carried out at the monasteries.

To return to the case of the donations that help support these institutions, the act of giving money or material resources generates a large amount of karmic merit for the donor. However, through the influence of Buddhist teachings on selflessness, the merit thus accumulated is not kept for the donor's individual advantage but is typically given away to others. Sometimes, the merit might be given to members of the donor's family for specific reasons (e.g., recovering from illness), but usually merit is dedicated for "the benefit of all sentient beings" via a ritual chant performed at the time of donation. A similar dedication is made at the end of meditation sessions in monasteries, hence ensuring that the monks and nuns do not undermine their progress toward liberation through the accumulation of karma for personal benefit.

That said, in line with merit's self-multiplying tendencies, even giving away merit is itself a meritorious act. The monastic-lay economic circuit is, we might say, a hyper-productive karmic engine—donating to the monastery produces merit, practicing at the monastery produces merit, and giving all this merit away produces yet more merit. To invoke Bataille's language, vast stores of unclaimed merit are freely squandered for the benefit of all sentient beings. Indeed, merit can only be "extravagant," according to Bataille's use of this term—due to its tendency to multiply at an immeasurable rate, it can never be calculated according to the logic of any restricted economic system.

In instances of interactions across money economies and merit economies, such as donations to temples, we witness the instability of restricted systems; but, it is important to note, this instability is not driven by an impending "catastrophic" breakdown, as Bataille tends to emphasize, but by the effect of compassion, which has the power to disrupt any limited calculation of exchange. Restricted economies are indeed unstable, but the principle of general economy acquires a different complexion when cast in light of Buddhist compassion. In the spirit of Bataille's own case studies, three examples serve to illustrate the "extravagance" of compassion in relation to the distinction between restricted and general economies, as well as to prepare us for the "existential Buddhism"[17] of the Korean nun Kim Iryŏp in the last half of the chapter. Below we will consider (1) contemporary Theravāda temple practices, (2) a Sui-dynasty Mahāyāna movement eventually banned by the Chinese government, and (3) long-standing beliefs regarding the power of Amitābha Buddha's altruism to intervene in restricted karmic exchanges.

To begin, consider the standard temple practices related to soliciting and managing donations. In a 2005 article, anthropologist Jiemin Bao discusses merit-making rituals at a contemporary Silicon Valley temple serving a Thai population.[18] At the temple, visitors may purchase gift baskets for the monks ranging from 10 to 150 dollars apiece and containing various useful items such as soap, canned food, and, at the more expensive end, extra robes. The purchaser of such a basket then presents it personally to the monk in a common merit-producing ritual. At the Silicon Valley temple, as at others, very often the baskets are never opened; rather, they remain inside their cellophane wrappers, to be put back out on the sales table and sold again.[19] This is not deception—everyone involved knows that the baskets are resold. The purchasers are interested in making merit, so the important act is the formal presentation of the basket to the monk. In return for facilitating this merit ritual, the temple receives revenue that it uses not only to support the monks but to fund a variety of events and services that generate positive outcomes for the community. The benefits of karmic merit-production are, in this case, palpable in the material world.

As such, these commonplace temple practices mark a moment of contact between a money economy and a merit economy. And, in this moment, we see the capability of merit rituals to tinker in the normal mechanics of monetary exchange, accomplishing transactions that money economies do not ordinarily allow—e.g., enabling a static lump sum of principle (the gift baskets) to generate revenue perpetually. As the case of the Thai temple indicates, real-world finances are transformed through merit production. Perhaps an even more extravagant example of such transformation is the now-defunct Sanjie or "three stages" movement, which arose in China around the turn of the Sui dynasty (581–618). Its founder, the Mahāyāna Buddhist monk Xinxing (540-94), taught that incalculable quantities of merit were generated by a single donation to the Sanjie community. On the one hand, Sanjie institutions employed the usual system of exchanging money for merit seen at the Silicon Valley temple. On the other hand, in the Sanjie context, the donated capital did not simply accrue to the monastery; rather, anyone could borrow from the store of money and resources as needed, and repayment was optional and interest-free.[20] The Sanjie system was, by some measures, a wild success—it amassed such wealth that it began to rival the government. As Wendi Adamek says, it "abrogated state-like functions: relief for the needy and redistribution of wealth."[21] This state-like power was likely a factor in its eventual demise at the hands of the ruling elite.[22]

Though the Sanjie sect is long gone, the majority of Mahāyāna lineages in East Asia today—i.e., those which have come to be referred to collectively as Pure Land Buddhism—are similarly premised on the power of radical altruism to intervene in karmic conditions. Pure Land teachings are rooted in the Longer Sukhāvatīvyūha Sūtra, which tells of a king who lived eons before the time of Śākyamuni. This king became the bodhisattva Dharmakāra and then, after hundreds of years of meditation, the buddha Amitābha. Upon his attainment of full buddhahood, Amitābha generated a "buddha-field" (*buddhakṣetra*), indicating the realm of his influence. Early uses of this term in Buddhist cosmology referred to a single world-system, replete with multiple planes of existence, which constituted the realm or "buddha-field" of Śākyamuni Buddha. However, as the notion of a buddha's sphere of influence began to take more concrete form, the single-world cosmology blossomed into a multiverse of incalculable world-systems, each containing at most a single buddha.[23]

Amitābha's buddha-field, or Sukhāvatī, is known in East Asian Mahāyāna schools as the "pure land" (Ch. *jingtu* 淨土) where devotees can be reborn thanks to Amitābha's vow to allow entry to anyone who calls his name. He fulfills this vow via a donation from the incalculable store of merit that he gained over numerous lifetimes leading up to his attaining of buddhahood. Amitābha's realm is famously luxurious, where inhabitants are free of physical pain, and where they all benefit from ample time to devote themselves to Buddhist practice under the tutelage of a great liberated being. After attaining enlightenment themselves, they are reborn in the human realm to help other beings. This fulfills the "bodhisattva path," which is a characteristic feature of Mahāyāna lineages—a bodhisattva commits to remain within the cycles of death and rebirth until all sentient beings are liberated from suffering.

Shinran (1173–1263), the founder of the largest Pure Land school in Japan today, puts special emphasis on the impossibility of "earning" our way toward liberation through the accumulation of karmic merit generated via our own good deeds or Buddhist practices. In the *Tannishō*, a record of Shinran's teachings attributed to a student

Yuien, Shinran is reported to have said: "It is impossible for us, who are possessed of blind passions, to free ourselves from birth-and-death through any practice whatever. Sorrowing at this, Amida [Amitābha] made the Vow, the essential intent of which is the evil person's attainment of Buddhahood."[24] Here, it is the sorrow of Amitābha that intervenes in the usual karmic order and disrupts any simplistic understanding in which the merit we accumulate will benefit us, and the bad karma we produce will harm us. In one of Yuien's comments in the *Tannishō*, he explains that Amitābha's merit transfer (Jp. *eko* 回向) does not operate according to a system of straightforward economic exchanges: "[Shinran] spoke of how we believe that if our hearts are good, then it is good for birth, and if our hearts are evil, it is bad for birth, failing to realize that it is by the inconceivable working of the Vow that we are saved."[25] On the one hand, Amitābha did "earn" his store of merit over lifetimes of practice; on the other, his unceasing altruism fuels that merit's perpetual increase—he is *constantly* squandering it on us deluded beings. In this sense, his merit transfer seems to be both inside and outside the karmic order, operative within it but not bound to its logic of exchange. We might say, then, that the power of Amitābha's altruism is subversive, in that it destabilizes or unsettles the flow of karmic back-and-forth.

In a recent book on Pure Land and leftist politics in twentieth-century Japan, Melissa Anne-Marie Curley notes Amitābha's ability to subvert the karmic order that governs death and rebirth, and she links this to later political movements that use Pure Land rhetoric to intervene in the social order that governs the human world. Various ritual recitations of Amitābha's name effectively guarantee rebirth in the Pure Land not as a future event but as an immediate transformation: "by reorganizing the elements of the phenomenal world in the shape of the otherworldly Pure Land, they make present the moment of cathexis in which Amida grasps the practitioner and carries him or her to the Pure Land .... as sites of cathexis, they destabilize the real world, interrupting the real social order."[26] As she concludes, this ability to intervene in real social conditions explains why early Japanese leftists found inspiration in the Pure Land not only as an image for socialist utopia but as a program for enacting that utopia in the present world.

As these examples show, karmic economies can interact with money economies, can spawn religious movements, and can function as drivers of social change. The rampant proliferation of karmic merit, from this perspective, is simultaneously the production of new values that directly affect human societies and cultures. Discussing the role of merit in the lives of Japanese Zen Buddhists, T. Griffith Foulk comments: "It is as real to them as, say, money—that other symbolic, magical thing that has no substantial existence but nevertheless serves to organize human societies and get things done."[27]

Our Existential Condition in a Karmic Economy

Merit may indeed serve as a driver of new values, but where does all this leave us, in terms of our existential questions? In the Buddhist multiverse, the karmic economy is not the result of any god's design. Śākyamuni Buddha never addresses the questions of why karma functions as it does or how it originates. In fact, he says that there is no perceivable beginning to the "whole mass of suffering" in which we are caught: "A first point is not discerned of beings roaming and wandering on hindered by ignorance and fettered by craving."[28] Because of the interdependent and cyclical nature of karmic causality, it would not be possible, as he explains, to trace the heritage of a single being back along a linear path to arrive at some "first cause."[29]

Likewise, meaningfulness in the Buddhist worldview is not framed in terms of any divine destiny. As already noted, the ultimate mortality of fully liberated beings is left a mystery, but even liberation itself is not understood as the goal or purpose of human life. Or, to put it another way, liberation is a response to the conditions in which we find ourselves, not the reason these conditions exist in the first place. This all speaks to what is perhaps Buddhism's most notable existential insight—i.e., impermanence, or the claim that all existing forms are temporary. This applies not just to living beings but to whole worlds and world-systems. Even the Buddhist heavens and hells are but temporary constructions held in place only so long as karmic causes and conditions can sustain them. Bataille, in this sense, was right—all restricted systems of meaning are ultimately subject to decay. In the words of the twentieth-century Korean nun Kim Iryŏp, "Emptiness performs the dual activities of construction and dissolution from eternity to eternity without end."[30]

However, this is not to say that the Buddhist multiverse lacks value. The alleviation of suffering, in any form, serves as the standard by which all "good" and "bad" conditions are judged. Through the forces of karma that link us all together, we co-create worlds of meaning that set the terms of both our bondage and our liberation. Perhaps no Buddhist writer better communicates this capacity for creativity within the karmic economy than Kim Iryŏp.

As we will see in what follows, Iryŏp's writings orient the existential dilemmas of our karmic cycles in terms of Mahāyāna non-dualism, that is, the radical non-difference between self and other, form and emptiness, even "inner" mind and "external" world. According to Mahāyāna Prajñāpāramitā or "perfection of wisdom" teachings, the doctrine of no-self means that there is no "self" to liberate from suffering. Therefore, there can be no fundamental difference between suffering and liberation, delusion and enlightenment, or buddhas and ordinary beings. All existing forms persist only through their mutual interdependence and are fundamentally empty on their own. As Iryŏp says, "The greatest truth is the greatest contradiction .... The Buddha and the devil are one, and sentient beings and the Buddha are not dual."[31] These core Mahāyāna ideas of *emptiness* and *non-dualism* underlie all of Iryŏp's existential thought, marking a departure from the dilemmas of subject–object duality we saw in the earlier chapter.

Kim Iryŏp's Existential Buddhism

Kim Iryŏp was born Kim Wonju in 1878 and achieved notoriety in the 1920s as a feminist author and activist.[32] Then, in a move that was surprising to many at the time, she joined a Buddhist nunnery in 1933 and remained a nun until her death in 1971. Through her conversion to Buddhism, she took the dharma-name Iryŏp. She was ordained in the Korean Seon tradition of Mahāyāna Buddhism, which is perhaps better known as Zen in the West (both Korean Seon and Japanese Zen derive from the Chinese Chan 禪 lineage).

Iryŏp describes her turn to monasticism as a kind of existential emergency—from a place of deep confusion and emotional unrest, she found that only Buddhism offered the key to true peace and authentic human freedom. As she says, unlike other religions such as Protestantism and Catholicism, "The Buddha taught the law of causality, the understanding of which leads one to the path of independence."[33] As we have already seen, this law of causality explains the basic mechanisms by which the self both falls prey to suffering and attains liberation. For Iryŏp, this law operates in humans at the most basic level: "Human beings primarily consist of the material mind that senses joy and sorrow."[34] This is the mind that acts and reacts, that negates and affirms, and that feels desire and repulsion. When we blindly chase our desires down the corridors of the mind, we become lost in our own attachments, through which we build up a limited but cohesive sense of self. We remain ensnared in our desires until we see through the ego to what Iryŏp calls the "mind of nothingness," which opens us to the full potential of our humanity: "Only when we live according to the 'mind of nothingness' ... which is the thought before a thought arises, does life as a human being begin."[35]

Here Iryŏp's language reflects the rhetoric of the Chan Buddhist school to which her nunnery belonged.[36] For example, the great Chan patriarch Huineng (638–713) speaks of liberation in terms of the "original nature" (Ch. *benxing* 本性) or "original mind" (*benxin* 本心) that resides in a state of "no-thought" (*wunian* 無念).[37] He explains: "If you see all things without the mind being affected or attached, that is 'no thought.' Its function pervades everywhere, without being attached anywhere .... coming and going freely, comprehensively functioning without stagnation ... That is the practice of 'no thought.'"[38] He cautions that no-thought (*wunian* 無念) does not mean "not thinking" (*busi* 不思)[39] or a simple state of non-awareness, warning meditators not to be "fixated on indifferent voidness."[40] Instead, the original mind is capacious and dynamic, like the universe itself:

> Good friends, the universe is empty, and so contains the colors and forms of myriad things, the sun, moon, and stars, the mountains, rivers, and land, the springs and valley streams, the grasses, trees, and forests, bad people and good people, bad things and good things, heaven and hell, the oceans and the mountain—all are in emptiness. All these are possible because of emptiness. The emptiness of the essential nature of people in the world is also like this. Good friends, our inherent nature can contain all things—this is greatness.[41]

Building on these Chan insights, Iryŏp speaks with urgency about the necessity of every single human being realizing such "greatness," which, she says, enables the full potential of human powers.

Observing people around her who remain ensnared in the small-minded ego, Iryŏp frequently compares them to "dolls." They are like robots or zombies—they go through the motions of doing and acting, but they do not truly *do* anything, because they are neither free nor in control of themselves. Iryŏp is clear that there can be no social change in a society of mindless dolls. She says: "How, then, do we find the complete self? This is the big issue. Only when this urgent issue is resolved do we finally become human beings; only when we become human beings does the life of a human being begin; and only then will we be able to think about family life, social responsibilities, and so on."[42] Accordingly, after entering the monastery, Iryŏp devotes herself fully to Buddhist practice and ceases her activities as a literary author and political activist, refraining from reading and writing for over ten years. The translator of Iryŏp's writings, Jin Y. Park, comments: "On the surface Kim Iryŏp appears to have lived two distinct lives."[43] But Park also cautions against taking a simplistic view of Kim's engagement with both feminist politics and Buddhism.

The simplistic account of Iryŏp's life would imply that she spends her younger years as a writer and social activist, and then, at a key turning point, she realizes that social change is not possible until after our existential dilemmas have been addressed. After this realization, she retreats to a nunnery and works on her own existential liberation. After a long period of asceticism, she emerges from her seclusion with new writings, exhorting everyone to follow her lead—i.e., first to work privately toward existential liberation (ideally, through sustained monastic practice) and, only after that, to come together again and work toward social progress.

There is certainly evidence in Iryŏp's writings that this simplistic account might be correct. For example, she says, "An ordained person completes her education at a monastery and thus learns how to fully utilize the independent mind …. Having realized the independent mind, she can return to the secular world and live free from the dualities."[44] Elsewhere, she says, "What is urgent at this point is to build meditation halls everywhere, to provide places to practice …. World peace and human freedom will be accomplished when each nation makes the effort to see that each individual becomes a true human being."[45] Such passages do seem to indicate that Iryŏp is instructing people to work on their own existential liberation before returning to a life of social activism.

However, upon closer analysis, this simplistic account positions Iryŏp's ideas within the dualistic logic of subject and object, and such logic runs counter to the basic Buddhist doctrines that she consistently advocates. In particular, the simplistic account assumes that human beings are separate entities, and that society is formed when a collection of such entities come together. By this reasoning, if we gather together a group of mindless dolls, then we will have an unhealthy society; and if we gather together a group of true human beings, we will have an enlightened one. It may be tempting to assume that Iryŏp prioritizes monastic practice before social activism due to such reasoning, but nothing in her writings suggests that this is how she believes either individuals or social groups function. She repeatedly adheres to the radical non-duality of Mahāyāna Buddhism, saying, for example, that a single person is "the whole of the embodiment of the universe," that the arising of a single thought is the arising of the entire cosmos, or that a single grain of sand is "the very unity composing the entire body of the universe."[46] Given this non-dualist standpoint, it seems unlikely that Iryŏp would believe that separate individuals should first transform themselves privately and later come together to form a group.

In a more complicated account of Iryŏp's politics, when she retreats to the monastery, she is not taking a break from activism or setting aside her commitment to the women's liberation movement. Rather, her monastic practice itself is a force for social change. This statement makes sense if we recall the earlier comment that monasteries are "hyper-productive karmic engines" that link the lives of laypeople to the practices of monks and nuns. The extravagant quantities of karmic merit generated by the monasteries promote, in the long run, liberation from karma altogether. As Iryŏp says, "A free individual [is] relieved of the constraints of karma, living as the controller of her original mind, of which she is the master."⁴⁷ Much like Amitābha and his merit transfer that operates both inside and outside the karmic system, the one who acts as "master" of herself exists in the karmically conditioned world but is "relieved of the constraints of karma"—i.e., her actions are not subsumed within the existing karmic order but instead have the potential to change it, thereby opening up a path toward liberation for others, as well. The meritorious meditation of the nun can affect the entire karmic network that sustains the societal conditions in which she is located.

This is entirely in line with standard Mahāyāna accounts of the potential for selfless action to subvert, circumvent, or otherwise thwart the seemingly iron-clad law of karmic reward and punishment, as in the example of Amitābha's vow to grant ordinary beings rebirth in Sukhāvatī. The meritorious activities of monks and nuns, when accomplished from the standpoint of selflessness, do not benefit simply the individual practitioners but, to the contrary, reverberate through myriad interconnected karmic networks to palpably impact worldly conditions. From this perspective, it is clear that Iryŏp does not view life in the monastery as a retreat from the world or an abandonment of her commitment to social change. To the contrary, as we will see in the next section, she believes that monastic activity enables superhuman powers on the scale of Amitābha Buddha, granting us the freedom to intervene in karmic processes and create whole worlds of meaning.

Iryŏp and Value-Creation

Emptiness is absolute and includes everything. It is justice, truth, and authenticity. Action taken in emptiness is rightness; eyes that see through emptiness are correct; ears that hear through emptiness never comprehend inaccurately. Emptiness is seamless, without the slightest gap; it is filled with all things, even the unimaginable.

—*Kim Iryŏp*⁴⁸

Although Iryŏp never exits the basic Buddhist framework, she nonetheless uses atypical terminology to express her own unique philosophical perspective on the meaning of Mahāyāna emptiness. For example, in a somewhat unexpected turn of phrase, she describes the mind of nothingness as "action": "Action is the other side of thought; this action is the thought before a thought arises."[49] Her formulation reminds us that, unlike those dolls who have lost their minds, only the true self is capable of acting freely and efficaciously in the world. She continues this line of inquiry in a fascinating essay titled "Buddhism and Culture," where she describes a buddha as "a great person of culture."[50] She explains her ideas in terms of "the mind of nothingness" or "the other side of thought," here described specifically as "creativity" (K. *ch'angjosŏng*):

> The person of culture is a creator who constructs all forms of existence. The person of culture first becomes aware of her own creativity, which is equipped with all the cultural assets needed to attain power for creative activities (which is to attain awakening).... this creativity, which I have identified as the cultural capacity of each individual, is the other side of thought.[51]

As this shows, the small self may be determined by karmic causes and conditions, and in that sense, it is mostly a product of its culture. The great self, in contrast, is a creator of culture who, as she says above, "constructs all forms of existence." This is clearly *not* a matter of an isolated subject projecting values onto the world—Iryŏp has something more in mind.

Should we understand Iryŏp in a Niezschean sense to mean that the great self is the creator of new values? She certainly shares affinities with Nietzsche's existentialism, but her notion of "creativity" is best understood within the Buddhist karmic economy in which she herself locates her philosophy. As we saw above, due to the basic truth of non-duality to which Iryŏp adheres, personal transformation is simultaneously the transformation of the wider karmic network in which all beings are located. In this light, for Iryŏp, "creativity" means specifically the power of selfless action to transform karmic conditions. To quote her at length, she says:

> When we say oneness, concreteness, or representation, we are referring to the actual, concrete reality that is one's own self, the self that does not have an outside. When one owns something, one uses it within its limitations; when one says "I," this "I" is a concrete reality, the reality one is fully in charge of. Since the created and the creator are not two different entities, this great dharma hall [of Sudŏk Monastery], which is a work of art by a person of the Way, is the creation of someone fully in charge of himself. The creator can create a mountain or water and he can make them come or go. This is possible because the subject and object become one when the subject "I" is completely free.[52]

Iryŏp's notion of "concrete reality" immediately rejects the dualism of inner self and external world by describing the self as having no "outside." Reality knows no split into subject and object. For Iryŏp, inner transformations ("a person of the Way") and outer manifestations (the dharma hall at Sudŏk Monastery) are one and the same—both the dharma hall and its maker are expressions of the same action of selfless creativity. This creativity, via the concrete items of material culture such as Sudŏk Monastery, establishes the Buddhist world of meaning far and wide. The important distinction is not between subject and object but between those subjects who are at the mercy of karmic conditions and those who have attained freedom and hence the power to create.

These ideas of both non-dual interconnectedness and creativity seem crucial to understanding Iryŏp's later writings on "life energy" (K. *saengmyŏng*), which again take Buddhist rhetoric in her own unique direction. In this work, Iryŏp uses the term "life energy" where she was earlier using terms such as "great self" or "complete person" or "original mind." For example, she says: "Life energy is omnipotent and exists before things exist; it does not have a visible shape and yet is all-capable. The existential value of a living organism lies in its capacity to attain life energy and utilize that energy at its will."[53] Invoking a tree metaphor, she says that life energy, although formless, is the root and trunk of all life. In contrast, the stems and branches on the tree have forms, which are shaped through the accumulation of karma: "A group of sentient beings whose karma is similar in nature comprise a stem and live in the same universe."[54] On this metaphor, to change karmic conditions quite directly affects the very form that life energy has taken—it is structural change on a universal scale.

In this metaphor, on the one hand, we see the Mahāyāna interplay between emptiness and form: life energy, which is synonymous with emptiness, is the formless root of all life; and life, in the form as we know it and live it, is shaped by karmic conditions. On the other hand, we see Iryŏp's idiosyncratic description of emptiness as a kind of energy that can be utilized to creatively transform both self and world. Iryŏp says:

> Emptiness is the foundation of all things; hence, once you attain emptiness, there is nothing you cannot do. A being is more properly called a beast who does not know that emptiness is the self ... and thus fails to utilize this emptiness. A great artisan knows how to mold things ... likewise the Buddha or God refers to the being that is capable of fully grasping emptiness and utilizing it to its utmost. To take refuge in the Buddha or God ... is thus to live as the artist-creator of the universe.[55]

This "artist-creator" can transform the conditions around her, her culture, her very reality, through the radical creativity of emptiness.

How is such power attained? Meditation, says Iryŏp, is the practice that enables our creativity by cultivating the life energy that affects both self and other: "The only answer is meditation (meditation means cultivation, and cultivation is a way to recover one's self, which is the original mind of each individual, which is creativity, and which is the self in which self and others are united)."[56] Here we return to our earlier point that, for Iryŏp, monastic practice is not a private affair. It is not a break from politics but is itself a force for social change, conducting a potent energy that reaches out and transforms the karmic conditions in which many selves are united. Recalling the familiar feminist slogan that "the personal is political," for Iryŏp, we might say instead that "practice is political."

Of course, we might also respond, somewhat cynically, that this all sounds like magic—i.e., the idea of a meditator generating emptiness as a force to change the world around her. And, indeed, Iryŏp does say: "What people call supernatural powers or miracles are activities of those who have attained true humanhood and thus utilize their full capacities."[57] Perhaps modernist sensibilities might encourage us to dismiss Iryŏp's ideas about superhuman powers and pervasive life-energies, but nonetheless I am interested in taking Iryŏp seriously. What if structural change, in the sociopolitical sense, does demand of us radical personal transformation? What if the power to "create values" and shape the conditions around us does require a dedicated and life-consuming practice such as Iryŏp's monasticism?

So far, only Iryŏp's existentialism via Buddhism seems to be effectively disentangled from the subject–object framework, in which people collectively project the figment of subjective meaning onto an inert objective world. In other words, it is so far only Iryŏp who makes the outrageous claim that individual beings are caught up in the manifestation of reality itself and can exert some influence over its production. On this point, Iryŏp's ideas certainly resonate with the existential theories of Nietzsche and Beauvior, who cast humans as meaning-makers and value-creators. But I suspect that Iryŏp would consider their theories incomplete without a more robust account of the practices, like meditation, that enable such creative potential to be fully utilized.

From Karmic Law to Cosmic Mandate

Ultimately, then, Iryŏp does indeed give us an account of value creation—we all participate in the co-creation of "good" and "bad," of conditions that are "better" and "worse," of whole worlds of meaning, through the force of our own activity. For Iryŏp, the related ideas of non-duality and karmic interconnectedness provide a coherent causal framework in which to understand these processes. The karmic network can explain both how preexisting social and cultural conditions impact the construction of the self and how a meditator's own liberatory transformation can, in turn, impact the conditions around her. But, from outside this Buddhist cosmology, the mechanism of karma may seem mysterious.

Iryŏp's later writings on "life energy" or "life force" help to link her existential insights to a wider range of East Asian discourses. The term for "life energy," *saengmyŏng*, is taken from the Chinese *shengming* (生命) and is not particularly Buddhist at all; rather, it is a concept related to long-standing and pervasive assumptions about life (*sheng* 生), energy (*qi* 氣), and the cosmos (*tian* 天)[58] in traditional Chinese thought—assumptions that affect areas as diverse as medicine, architecture, and the arts, in addition to philosophy. Indeed, Iryŏp's description of emptiness as a kind of formless life-energy situates her in a long line of East Asian thinkers, Buddhist and Ruist alike, who speak of emptiness not as utter nothingness but as an inchoate, primal, creative source.

For example, as she says, in language that is, to stress again, not particularly Buddhist: "The Buddha and God penetrate the meaning of emptiness and create a universe using emptiness as its material."[59]

What could it possibly mean to use emptiness as material? One clue lies in her comment, only a few passages later: "emptiness is not voidness …. Reality is what is thought of; the original body of reality is what comes before thought. Because the original body has no visible shape, it is called empty."[60] As we will see in what follows, Iryŏp here aligns with a number of strands of Ruist thought that reject the metaphysical plausibility of utter nothingness. According to these traditions, what is called "empty" (*wu* 無) in fact refers to what is empty of form or "formless" (*wuxing* 無形). In the matter–energy matrix of *qi*-cosmology, formless primordial *qi* is indeed the material out of which whole universes are created. Kim Iryŏp is certainly a dedicated Buddhist practitioner, but her existential thought reflects the syncretism that has long characterized Buddhism, Daoism, and Ruism in East Asia, and so it is to these latter traditions that the next chapter turns.

3

The Creation of New Values, Part II: Cosmic Correspondences

In the ancient past, when Lord Bao Xi ruled over everything under the sun, he looked up to contemplate the images in the sky, and he looked down to contemplate the forms on earth. He contemplated the patterned appearances of birds and animals, as well as the suitability of their habitats. He examined his own body up close, as well as things at a distance. Thus he devised the Eight Hexagrams, in order to convey the power of spiritual clarity and to classify the conditions of myriad things.

—Commentary on the appended phrases of the Book of Changes[1]

Author and philosopher Milan Kundera speculates that an "existential mathematics, which does not exist, would probably propose this equation: the value of coincidence equals the degree of its improbability."[2] In his novel *The Unbearable Lightness of Being*, a young woman falls in love with a stranger after the universe supplies her with an improbable series of signs: Beethoven (her favorite) is playing in the café where she first sees him; his hotel room number (six) is the same as the house number of her childhood home; he sits on a bench in the park that she often visits; and he reads a book, she herself being an avid reader. In Kundera's hands, such fortuities take on a lyrical significance: "It is wrong, then, to chide the novel for being fascinated by mysterious coincidences ... but it is right to chide man for being blind to such coincidences in his daily life. For he thereby deprives his life of a dimension of beauty."[3]

But Kundera also provides a counterpoint to such lyricism. After some time has passed and the novel's central relationship has soured, the man reflects on the absurdity of his ever having met his lover in the first place:

> Seven years earlier, a complex neurological case *happened* to have been discovered at the hospital in Tereza's town …. the chief surgeon of Tomas's hospital *happened* to be suffering from sciatica, and … sent Tomas to the provincial hospital in his place. The town had several hotels, but Tomas *happened* to be given a room in the one where Tereza was employed. He *happened* to have had enough free time before his train left to stop at the hotel restaurant. Tereza *happened* to be on duty, and *happened* to be serving Tomas's table. It had taken six chance happenings to push Tomas towards Tereza, as if he had little inclination to go to her on his own.[4]

Who is right? Was the universe speaking to Tereza and Tomas? Or was there only a series of unrelated coincidences? Recall from the second chapter that David Hume expresses skepticism regarding our mind's habitual tendency to find meaningful connections where there are none. The fact that one event regularly follows another, he says, does not necessarily mean that the first event caused the second. I may be led to infer a causal relationship, especially if I encounter the series of two events on a regular basis; but ultimately I am unable to tell whether my habitual predictions regarding cause-and-effect are anything other than ungrounded speculations. This is what has come to be termed as philosophy's "problem of induction."

So much of our so-called meaning in life seems to suffer a similar problem, arising by inference based on the co-occurrence of two events. At one end of the induction spectrum, we have Hume's radical skepticism over even the most basic of meaningful connections—causality. At the other end, we have, perhaps, the Tarot card reader, who sees meaningful connections arising unchecked from the most improbable of sources, like Tereza's romantic numerology.

But here, I wish to challenge precisely the above characterization of this spectrum of induction, which relies on the now-familiar idealist–realist debate: Is meaning created by subjects or discovered "out there" in the objective world? Is a coincidence "really meaningful" or "all in my head"? In the chapter that follows, we will consider that meaning is neither created nor discovered but rather *enacted*—it is produced via the pursuit of microcosmic–macrocosmic correspondences that are simultaneously mental and material. Three key terms from Chinese philosophy are especially important to this existential investigation: *qi* (氣), the matter–energy matrix that characterizes existence as such, as well as all existing things; *li* (理), the patterns or structural tendencies of *qi* that account for the emergence, maintenance, and disintegration of its various manifestations; and *de* (德), the transformative power that enables structural stability as well as change, both spontaneously, through the dynamism of *qi* itself, and human-made, through our purposeful interventions. In the course of investigating the role of these terms in a variety of Chinese discourses below, a general trend emerges: we see that "new values" are not created, as it were, ex nihilo, but instead are forged through the radical transformation of old values with what we can call "techniques of realization."

The Matter–Energy Matrix of *Qi*

The Song-dynasty philosopher Zhu Xi (1130–1200) is one of the most influential figures in the history of Chinese thought. He amended the canon of core Chinese texts to include not only the Five Classics but also the so-called Four Books, which he established together as the basis of the civil service exam, which itself served as the gatekeeper to political power until the ailing Qing dynasty discontinued it in 1905. His editorial interventions in the canon and his philosophical commentaries on the core texts occupied mainstream Chinese philosophy for centuries. As we will see later, Zhu is but one figure in a much larger cast of philosophers who can be said to be the creators of new values in Chinese history—although the meaning of "creation" in this context needs further explanation and will be taken up later. We begin here with Zhu's extensive writings on the nature of the "heart-mind" or our capacities for "thinking-and-feeling" (*xin* 心).

In a detailed study of these writings, the contemporary philosopher Eiho Baba discusses the mental activity of *zhijue* (知覺). The term is often translated as "perception," having connotations of conscious awareness, intellectual thought, comprehension, and understanding. But, as Baba makes clear, *zhijue* is not simply a faculty of the mind but also an active element in the surrounding environment. Making sense of Zhu Xi's use of this term requires that we put on hold common assumptions about the relationship between inner subjective experiences and external environmental conditions. On the one hand, the Chinese tradition certainly recognizes the phenomenon of private experience—specific conditions are felt as sensations or apprehended as thoughts by a single person, such that these are not immediately visible, audible, or palpable to other people. On the other hand, these very sensations and thoughts are classified as types of fluid energies that reside within and move through the body; because they are not categorically different from the congealed energies that constitute physical matter, such "inner" forces can indeed become palpable to others externally, or serve as efficacious agents of change in the surrounding world.

The term *qi* refers to the matter–energy matrix of fluid and congealed forces that underlies Song and post-Song philosophical sensibilities about the nature of reality, which is to say, the types of things and processes that exist, how they arise, how they interact, and how they can be manipulated. Theories about *qi* and its behaviors affect studies and practices in fields as diverse as medicine, architecture, pedagogy, and cosmology. In all cases, the *qi*-matrix is believed to be structured according to the nested polarities of *yin* (陰) and *yang* (陽), where *yin* refers to forces that settle and sink, that are dark and heavy, and that tend to condense; and *yang* refers to forces that rise or flow, that are clear and light, and that tend to disperse. No single phenomenon is *yin* or *yang* on its own but only in relation to other phenomena in specific contexts. For example, the condensed or turbid *qi* of physical matter is a *yin* force in relation to the *yang* force of the etheric or refined *qi* of human thoughts and sensations. Within any given *yang-qi* or *yin-qi* constitution, there are further *yin* and *yang* aspects. The two forces that Baba highlights in his study of *zhijue* are *hun* (魂) and *po* (魄)—the former is the *yang* aspect of incorporeal *qi* (*yang-qi*) and the latter the *yang* aspect of corporeal *qi* (*yin-qi*). As such, *hun* and *po* refer to the most rarefied or "spiritual" (*shen* 神) aspects of the human heart-mind and body, respectively.

Keeping all this in mind, we can begin to parse the following passage from Zhu Xi, quoted by Baba, describing the forces of *hun* and *po* in relation to the activity of *zhijue*:

> *Yin* presides over storage and reception and *yang* presides over movements and applications (*yunyong* 運用). In general, the ability to memorize is all due to what *po* stores and receives, but the movements and applications manifested outward are *hun*. These two thing-events are fundamentally inseparable from each other (*buxiangli* 不相離). What enables memorization is *po*, but what manifests outward must be *hun*. That which enables *zhijue* is *po*, but that which manifests *zhijue* outward is *hun*. Each of them belongs respectively to *yin* and *yang*, but within these *yin* and *yang* there are further *yins* and *yangs*.[5]

Here we see that *zhijue* is dependent upon memorization, which is described as a *yin*-process responsible for the heart-mind's ability to receive and retain what it learns. But via its *yang*-aspect, *zhijue* also "manifests outward" (*fachulai* 發出來). Because *zhijue* involves both aspects—reception and retention accompanied by outward dispersal—Baba translates it as "realization," which captures a sense of intellectual insight as well as constructive manifestation. He says: "*Zhijue*, therefore, is not a passive seeing, as it were, of a predetermined reality, but a participatory determination of the world through cultivated appreciations and realizations."[6] Realization is, in short, the process of manifesting reality.

One key feature of a general *qi*-based philosophy that enables such "realization" is the recursive behavior of *qi*, or its ability to interact with itself in its different phases to produce increasingly complex manifestations. For example, the forces of *hun* and *po* can be described as types of mental processes or aspects of human capacities, but they can also be described as distinct energies with their own dynamic agency. In fact, several Daoist traditions recognize no less than three *hun* and seven *po*, which develop in a human fetus at the third and fourth months of gestation, respectively.[7] Moreover, widespread Chinese beliefs regarding the afterlife attribute various species of ghosts and spirits to the continued existence of these different *hun* and *po* after bodily death. So when Baba emphasizes *zhijue* as a process of manifestation enabled by *hun* and *po*, this does not simply mean that a single human agent takes in information and then imposes its will on the external world; rather, a lively collection of animating forces can emanate from the subject to varying degrees and according to varying circumstances, sometimes under the influence of the conscious mind and sometimes not.

This is a key point to note: As with Kim Iryŏp's views on creativity in the previous chapter, here we see another deep affinity with Nietzsche, who also considered the human psyche to be a multiplicity. In *Composing the Soul*, a wide-ranging study of Nietzsche's psychological writings, Graham Parkes describes the psyche not as the possession of a single ego but as a collection of diverse drives with sometimes competing aims and desires.[8] In the case of Ruist thought, these diverse members of the psyche are, in a very interesting sense, unrestrained by the borders of the body. What should we make of this?

Indeed, as Yung Sik Kim explains, the recursive interactions of *qi* mean that an individual's mental life is not simply an internal experience, nor is it restricted to the confines of her physical body:

> Mind, for Zhu Xi, was really nothing but *qi*, its "essential and refreshing" (*jingshuang* 精爽) or "numinous" (*ling* 靈) portion, to be more specific. Thus, *qi* was endowed with qualities of mind, and could interact with the mind. The mind-*qi* interaction was not restricted to man's *qi* and his own mind, but was extended to the *qi* of the outside world and to the minds of others.[9]

However, not all people attain such access beyond the perspective of their own limited awareness. The Chinese tradition defines petty or "small" people (*xiaoren* 小人) as those who barely understand themselves, let alone the outside world and other people. In contrast, the sages (*shengren* 聖人) are those who have cultivated themselves to attain special powers of realization and manifestation. As Joseph Adler explains, "Only sages have minds that can penetrate and comprehend the totality of the natural/moral order. This ability also gives them 'talents,' such as precognition, that make them appear 'like spirits' to ordinary people."[10] In particular, as the *qi* of the sage's mind becomes increasingly refined, sensitive, and agile, the sage enters into extraordinary relations with the surrounding environment: "When the mind's capacity for psycho-physical intercourse with things … is developed to the highest degree, it is called 'spiritual' (*shen*), or 'spiritual clarity' (*shenming*)."[11]

We next consider various methods for developing spiritual clarity and other powers of the sage. Following Baba's work on *zhijue*, we focus on the two aspects of realization via techniques for memorization and manifestation.

Memorization as Self-Transformation

Zhu Xi adamantly believes that reciting and memorizing texts is the key first step to transforming the heart-mind, enabling even the petty person to become a sage. As he says, "The value of a book is in the recitation of it. By reciting it often, we naturally come to understand it."[12] He continues, in a speculative vein: "I don't know how the mind so naturally harmonizes with the *qi*, feels uplifted and energized, and remembers securely what it reads."[13] As this suggests, to read a book is to palpably imprint on the mind, and to memorize and recite that book, as a method of *qi*-cultivation, is to sustain those effects on the mind.

In line with Zhu Xi's views on *qi* and the nature of the heart-mind, he refers to dynamics such as vibration, resonance, and synchronization. He advises that we prepare ourselves, so that we may open our minds to the way a text itself resonates, even suggesting that we might sit still and hum as a method of "tuning in" to a text's meaning: "In reading, students must compose themselves and sit up straight, look leisurely at the text and hum softly, open their minds and immerse themselves in the words."[14] The most important techniques to open the mind for effective memorization involve meditative breathing and "quiet sitting" (*jingzuo* 靜坐), which cultivate a mirror-like mental state that easily receives and retains: "Presently, should you want to engage in book learning, you must first settle the mind so that it becomes like still water or a clear mirror."[15]

Meditative practices for settling the mind do not simply enable a student to correctly interpret the meaning of a particular text; they allow the student to be in synchrony with the "order," "coherence," or "structure" that a classical text transmits. As Zhu Xi says, "When the mind is not settled, it doesn't understand 'structure.'"[16] The word for "structure" or *li* (理) is a philosophical companion term to *qi*. As discussed above, the matter–energy matrix of *qi* exhibits certain self-organizing tendencies characterized by the polar relations of *yin* and *yang*. *Li* can refer to the overall self-organizing tendencies of the cosmos as well as the specific structures of individual things. It refers to mental structures, such as the interactions of *hun* and *po* that enable *zhijue*, as well as material ones, such as the cycles of the seasons or the behaviors of plants in an ecosystem. All these various systems (the heart-mind, the body, the world, the environment) express different levels of interrelated microcosmic and macrocosmic structures, which can, under optimal conditions, be productively attuned to each other. Most importantly for Zhu Xi, *li* refers to a moral order that aligns human society with the harmonious structures of the larger cosmos. Settling the mind through meditative practice is the first and most crucial technique, enacted at the microcosmic level, for aligning it with the moral order expressed in classic texts, and then manifesting this structure in the world.

Zhu Xi's beliefs about mental calm and effective learning are rooted in widespread and long-standing techniques for transformation and manifestation seen in numerous Chinese philosophical movements. The *Guanzi* (管子), a syncretic text dating back at least to the fourth century CE, provides us with practical insights into the third term needed to understand the transformative effects of learning and memorization, that is, *de* (德), translated as "virtue" or "power." This term is, of course, famously associated with the Daoist classic *Daodejing* (道德經), but the *Guanzi* contains some of the earliest known instructions for practices related to honing this "power." Like Zhu Xi, the *Guanzi* tells us, "Where the mind is still and the *qi* is well-structured [*xin jing qi li* 心靜氣理], there the way [*dao* 道] can be brought to rest."[17] It describes this state of mental stillness (*jing* 靜) as a calm and steady awareness, which we can train ourselves to maintain, even when events around us are chaotic. There are several techniques recommended, including breathing exercises, physical exercises, calming the mind by listening to appropriate music, and meditating to rid the mind of the accumulated beliefs that render it inflexible. Above all, the text says, *qi* cannot be well-structured through brute force but only through the transformative effects of power (*de*), which refers to *qi*'s natural tendencies to settle into its calm and clear, yet potent, state: "Therefore, regarding *qi*—it cannot be restrained by physical strength [*li* 力] but may be brought to rest by power [*de* 德]."[18] By acting in accord with the tendencies of *qi*, the sage is able to draw on powers larger than the individual's will or limited agency. This is why the actions of the sage are often described in terms of stillness, receptivity, and responsiveness.

In another passage, the *Guanzi* explains how the calm yet potent power of the sage aligns with larger structures in society and the cosmos:

> The reason it is called power [*de*] is that the sage is quick without moving, knows without being told, is successful without doing anything, and people arrive without being summoned. Such is the power. The cosmos does not move, yet the four seasons revolve below, and all things are transformed. The prince does not move, yet his government and orders function below, and all things are complete. The sage's mind does not move, yet it commands her four limbs, ears, and eyes, and in all things she is genuine."[19]

In this passage, we see the emergence of various still points—in the government, in the cosmos, and in the mind of the sage—that, when properly aligned, account for the efficacious functioning of all that exists. Here, power (*de*) refers to this transformative alignment that allows the effects of self-cultivation to reverberate up and down microcosmic and macrocosmic levels. The mind apprehends structure (*li*) thanks to this power, is transformed by this power, and thereby increases its own power to bring about transformations in larger social and environmental contexts.

Going back to Zhu Xi, all this begins with the *po*-aspect of our mental processes, which accounts for our ability to receive and retain structure via classical texts. However, this perhaps gives the impression that moral order is predetermined by cosmic fiat, transmitted through authoritative scriptures, and simply absorbed by the mind of the sage, like downloading software. In the next section, we turn to the productive and creative aspects of *zhijue*, which enable the manifestation of new value in the world.

Manifestation via Primordial *Qi*

Appreciating the sense in which moral structure is not deterministic will require a deeper look at the cosmology and cosmogony of *qi*. Most Ruist and Daoist traditions agree that *yin* and *yang* emerge from an originally undifferentiated field of *qi*, but there are disagreements as to whether the field itself emerged from a primal void or whether it has always existed, and whether the field of *qi* was initially chaotic or has always contained latent *yin-yang* order.[20] These unsettled questions are, I suggest, the persistent existential uncertainties of Chinese philosophical traditions. For present purposes, I am concerned not with resolving these uncertainties but with examining how Chinese traditions aim to flourish within them. In particular, we might note that primordial undifferentiated *qi* (*yuanqi* 元氣) is not only a feature of our cosmological origins but a force that remains with us in the present.[21] In other words, all existing forms emerge from undifferentiated *qi*, whether we are speaking of the first forms at the inception of the cosmos or the myriad forms around us now that continue to live out, in the present, ongoing processes of materialization, persistence, and eventual disintegration.

Under the right conditions, this primordial *qi* is available to us as a raw material, as it were, from which we can manifest or realize new forms, events, or processes—i.e., the *hun* aspect of *zhijue*. The ability to draw on this primal material is often portrayed as revitalizing, refreshing, and healthy. Going back to the *Guanzi*, we see both Daoist and Ruist resources brought in to discuss the efficacious practices of the wise ruler, who understands that flexibility and vitality are key to negotiating uncertain situations. In particular, some passages seem to align with a Daoist technique known as "fasting the mind" (*xinzhai* 心齋), a meditative process of clearing the mind of its accumulated forms so that its functioning remains supple and new forms may arise. The *Guanzi* warns: "It is ever so that the mind's form [*xing* 形], on being inundated with too much knowledge, loses its vitality [*sheng* 生]."[22] Elsewhere, the text links the flexible mind of the sage to his ability to draw on the wellspring of primal, undifferentiated *qi*, and thereby manifest structure: "Being extremely flexible is the way to respond to things …. Only the person of quality who grasps the primal unity is able to do this …. His sense of structure [*li*] is on a par with the universe."[23]

Overall, the *Guanzi* is confident on at least three points: (1) the practice of calming and clearing the mind has a reinvigorating effect; (2) the mind will spontaneously or naturally revert to its calm and clear state, without our needing to force it; and (3) the power of a well-regulated mind at the microcosmic level reverberates throughout higher levels, influencing bodily health, social harmony, and cosmic balance. However, what accounts for the power of the mind to spontaneously or naturally regulate itself? Here, the *Guanzi*'s answer is mysterious, though it seems to speak to the nested structure of microcosmic and macrocosmic isomorphism:

> The mind conceals a mind; within the mind there is another mind. In the mind's mind, thinking comes before sound. After thinking, there are forms. After forms, there are names. After names, there is utilization. After utilization, there is regulation. Without regulation, there is certainly chaos. With chaos, there is death.[24]

In a conspicuously high-stakes passage—certain death!—the manifestations of this "concealed mind" follow the pattern of cosmic manifestations leading from primordial *qi* to the proliferation of distinctions via forms and names, establishing an isomorphic correspondence between the concealed mind and the potency of undifferentiated *qi*. The text describes this as the "felt reality" or "phenomenological quality" (*qing* 情) of the mind that will spontaneously manifest when provided with "rest and quiet"; and it assures us that this state of mind is available whenever we call on it: "How clear! ... How nebulous! ... How expansive! ... It is never far away; we may daily use its power [*de*]."[25]

The general framework of *qi*-philosophy provides crucial context for understanding Kim Iryŏp's views on meditation that we saw at the end of the previous chapter. As Kim claimed, meditation is not simply a private experience but an efficacious practice that conducts transformative energy into the surrounding world. We can now see that her understanding of meditation reflects overarching East Asian views on *qi* as much as her Buddhist training. In fact, the three dominant philosophical traditions of East Asia—Ruism, Daoism, and Buddhism—seem to converge on a key point that has far-reaching implications for our existential engagement with the legacy of Nietzsche and the question of value-creation: namely, these traditions all agree that a creative power issues forth from the well-cultivated heart-mind of a sage or enlightened being.

In sum, in the Chinese context, the power of the mind to naturally attain its clear, nebulous, and expansive state is none other than the power of primordial *qi* to relinquish accumulated forms, nurture vitality, and continually renew and reinvigorate existence. The structure (*li*) of life as we know it is therefore not predetermined but constantly renegotiated. The polar tendencies of *yin* and *yang* serve as guidelines in this negotiation, not as fixed laws or foregone conclusions. This is nowhere so evident as in the most enigmatic of Chinese classical texts, the *Classic of Changes* or *Yijing* (易經). Despite Kundera's opening assertion, at the start of this chapter, that an "existential mathematics" does not exist, the *Yijing* nonetheless offers us advice on the accounting of meaning.

Realization as Divination

The Ming-dynasty philosopher Gao Panlong (1562–1626) describes a schedule for a one-day scholarly retreat, intended as a period of intellectual and spiritual renewal. His program includes periods of meditation, followed by periods of contemplative reading, punctuated by naps, walks, meals, gardening, and even a little rice wine at the end of the day. Right after the first morning meditation session, and before the first period of study, Gao instructs us to bathe, dress, burn some incense, and "play around" (*wan* 玩) with the *Yijing*.²⁶ His inclusion of the *Yijing* in this idyllic day of scholarship is not unique—most major Ruist philosophers from pre-Song times through the Ming and Qing dynasties memorized the *Yijing*, utilized it, and wrote commentaries on it. Perhaps due to its reputation as a divination system, like the Tarot, it has received much less scholarly attention in the West; but its prominent place in the history of Chinese philosophy, at the level of theory and practice, should be appreciated.

Earliest commentaries describe the text as a conduit for the same primal power that birthed the cosmos: "The *Book of Changes* contains the Great Ultimate; the Great Ultimate brings forth the Primordial Polarity; the Primordial Polarity brings forth the Four Images; and the Four Images bring forth the Eight Trigrams. These eight establish good fortune and misfortune. From fortune and misfortune comes forth the Great Life-Project."²⁷ According to the simplest explanation, the *Yijing* is a binary system of solid (—) and broken (- -) lines, which are arranged vertically into groups of three each, resulting in eight possible trigrams (*gua* 卦), which are then paired together to produce sixty-four possible hexagrams. Each hexagram has a name and is accompanied by a short, cryptic passage indicating its significance. Over time, these short passages have been explained and expanded through commentaries, and a canonical set of commentaries (the Ten Wings) is usually included as part of the *Yijing* proper. A person who consults the *Yijing* will use a variety of techniques to identify the hexagram or set of hexagrams relevant to a given situation, problem, or query.

In more complex terms, however, the *Yijing* is a training course for studying the behavioral tendencies of people and the general dynamics of interpersonal and environmental forces, drawing correspondences between microcosmic and macrocosmic structures, and identifying the best courses of action under specific conditions. In a comment that resonates with the existential focus here, Nicholas Brasovan observes: "In accordance with its structural complexity—the layers of textual interpretation, and its myriad allusions—the *Yijing* is a quintessential text for generating meaning."[28] As he goes on to explain, any single hexagram can be correlated with a variety of others through specific techniques—i.e., one hexagram easily transitions into another by swapping each individual line for its opposite or by reversing the order of the upper and lower trigrams. This tells us something not only about the logic of the *gua* but also about the tendencies of the phenomena associated with the hexagrams via the accumulated explanations and commentaries. As such, the hexagrams constitute an open-ended ecology of meaningful connections, as Brasovan describes:

> Each *gua* has a complex internal structure of interacting *yin* and *yang* lines, which can be referred to as a vertical dimension. At the same time, each *gua* is constituted by a complex set of relations to every other *gua* in the system, or a horizontal dimension. The interrelationships between *gua* are internal and constitutive, and are symbolic of the correlations that link actual phenomenon .... The idea, in other words, is that all events are porous; all events qua systems are open systems; all events are relatively particular and individual and relatively shared and environmental .... In line with their interconnection and principle of relativity, the set of hexagrams is seen as a parsimonious model—a cosmography—of the complex structure, and spontaneous and incessant change that is the world.[29]

An *Yijing* reading is a creative and productive hermeneutic exercise, as meaningful connections between the *gua* proliferate, and one insight leads to another down a path of interpretive inquiry that has no pre-determined end point.

Most importantly for our purposes, the study of the *Yijing* is not simply a method to transmit meaning (from the text to real life, or from past to present) but a practice for generating new meaning, as well. The historian Tze-Ki Hon identifies commentarial writing on the *Yijing* as the central vehicle for social and political reform in the Northern Song dynasty (960–1127):

> The Northern Song *Yijing* exegetes wrote their commentaries in response to the sociointellectual change of eleventh-century China, and as such, they contributed significantly to the establishment and functioning of civil governance. To different degrees, they were instrumental in fostering the political idealism of Northern Song civil bureaucrats who expressed their courage and imagination in full force in the drastic reforms of the mid- and late Northern Song. In hindsight, the civil bureaucrats might have overestimated their ability in establishing a perfect human order. However, even seen from today's perspective, their courage to envision a new sociopolitical system is admirable, and their ability to imagine the unimaginable is what makes the Northern Song so unique.[30]

What did Nietzsche expect the *Übermensch* to do, if not "imagine the unimaginable" so as to usher in a new age of humanity? A closer look at the Northern Song exegetes who are the subject of Hon's historical study opens a window on the practice of value-creation in the Chinese socio-political context.

Realization as Textual Commentary

Great commentarial traditions, such as the Talmud or the studies of Chinese classics, are not passive expositions of authoritative source materials but constructive and at times subversive projects, seizing the mainstream interpretations of influential texts and repurposing them for novel and creative applications.[31] New values are not produced, as said above, ex nihilo, but are wrested from the old values through techniques of realization, one of which involves manifesting meaning via commentarial writing.

In the early Song dynasty, China was emerging from a time of political unrest, marked by frequent periods of military rule, with power concentrated in the hands of aristocratic scholar-officials and passed down along hereditary lines. By the late Song, China had transitioned to an imperial system marked by relative stability, with power disbursed through more or less meritocratic means (i.e., public education and the civil service exam), managed by a progressive generation of civil bureaucrats who saw themselves as the rightful co-rulers of the common good.[32] Hon makes the convincing argument that this transfer of power from aristocratic families to the new generation of civil bureaucrats was aided, in large part, by creative commentarial writing that upended accepted interpretations of the classic texts, especially the *Yijing*. Hon begins with the *Yijing* commentary *Zhouyi kouyi* of the semi-hermit and later famed educator Hu Yuan (993–1059).

Hu boldly overturned the positions of several then-dominant *Yijing* commentaries[33] that, as he argued, were unduly influenced by Daoist notions of emptiness (*wu* 無), tended to overly romanticize hermits, and adopted a fatalistic attitude toward inevitable political unrest. Responding to the issue of emptiness, Hu rejected the notion that primal *qi* had emerged from an even more primal void, insisting there is always some state of *qi*, either "lacking-form" (*wuxing* 無形) or "having-forms" (*youxing* 有形).[34] But this seemingly obscure metaphysical point was indeed an act of political resistance. As Hon explains, by rejecting the theory of a primal void that transcends the world of forms, "Hu treated phenomenal affairs as ontologically real, and thereby significant in their own right."[35] In other words,

Hu returns emphasis to the concrete meaningfulness of the political affairs of his day and, much like Kim Iryŏp, makes political progress itself a function, and appropriate goal, of spiritual self-cultivation.

As such, the *Yijing*, in Hu's hands, is a text about the primordial reality of incessant change, which humans may navigate via the guiding principles of *yin* and *yang*, which directly affect the interplay between formed and formless *qi* and, in turn, directly construct our shared world. Later, Hon explains the political pay-off of this move:

> Whereas Kong Yingda's [much earlier] reading of the *Yijing* tended to support the absolute power of the king, underlying Hu Yuan's reading was his belief in human activism, directed broadly to all individuals.... He also believed that, as part of the universe, human beings were already fulfilling their cosmic mission by improving their social and political order. For him, since the universe is actively renewing itself with the interaction of the *yin* and the *yang*, human beings should also be actively renewing themselves in matters big and small.[36]

The means of renewal include, as above, cultivating the invigorating effects of primal formlessness accessible via the calm, clear, and settled mind. From the wellspring of the sage's heart-mind, new values are palpably manifested, by actions, by speech, and, as in this case, by subversive commentarial writing. As Hon makes clear, Hu's commentary on the *Yijing* was a decisive moment in the formation of the coherent social identity of the progressive civil bureaucrats of the late Song.[37]

Another influential *Yijing* exegete in Hon's study is Zhang Zai (1020–77), the uncle and philosophical colleague of the brothers Cheng Yi (1033–1107) and Cheng Hao (1032–85). All three were honored by Zhu Xi, who considered them his intellectual ancestors. Like Hu Yuan, Zhang Zai resists interpreting the *Yijing* in terms of the interplay between nothingness (*wu* 無) and existence (*you* 有). As he says: "If we realize that the Great Vacuity [*taixu* 太虛] is identical with *qi*, we know that there is no such thing as *wu* [無]."³⁸ This echoes Hu Yuan's interpretation that *wu* and *you* are best understood not as nothingness and existence per se but rather as the formless (*wuxing* 無形) and formed (*youxing* 有形) states of *qi*.

Also, as with Hu Yuan, Zhang Zai's views on *qi* deeply impacted his understanding of the *Yijing*'s socio-political relevance. In particular, in contrast to the mainstream commentaries that portrayed the *Yijing* as a political text, Zhang Zai presents it as a text on moral self-cultivation, linking it directly to the eight-step program of moral training outlined in the *Daxue* (大學) or "Great Learning" chapter of the classic text the *Book of Rites* (*Liji* 禮記). On the one hand, Hon himself points out that Zhang Zai's interpretation seems to be a stretch.³⁹ On the other hand, Zhang Zai's creative take on the *Yijing* has far-reaching consequences: The *Daxue* was the central text in Zhu Xi's educational reforms and a cornerstone of his overall philosophical movement. As mentioned above, Zhu still looms large in the intellectual history of China, often considered the founder of the Ruist renaissance known in Western scholarship as "neo-Confucianism." But when considered in historical context, he is one among a large cast of creators ushering in the new values of the Song.

We already saw part of the opening passage of the *Daxue* in the introductory chapter, but it bears repeating in full here:

> The way of great learning lies in illuminating luminous power, in renewing the people, and in coming to rest in utmost goodness. When you know where to rest, you can have stability. When you have stability, you can be tranquil. When you are tranquil, you can be at ease. When you are at ease, you can deliberate. When you deliberate, you can attain your aims. Things have their roots and branches; affairs have their end and beginning. When you know what comes first and what comes last, then you are near the way. The ancients, in wishing to illuminate luminous power in the world, first brought good order to their own states. Wanting to bring good

order to their states, they first regulated their households. Wanting to regulate their households, they first cultivated themselves. Wanting to cultivate themselves, they first corrected their minds. Wanting to correct their minds, they first made their intentions sincere. Wanting to make their intentions sincere, they first extended their knowledge. Extending knowledge consists in investigating things. Investigate things, and knowledge is extended. Extend knowledge, and intention becomes sincere. Make intention sincere, and the mind becomes correct. Correct the mind, and the self is cultivated. Cultivate the self, and the household is regulated. Regulate the household, and the state is brought to good order. Bring good order to the state, and the whole world will be at peace. From the ruler down to ordinary people, all must regard the cultivation of the self as the root.[40]

I follow Zhu Xi here (who follows Cheng Yi) in reading the verb in the second phrase as "renewing" (*xin* 新) and not "loving" (*qin* 親) the people.[41] Zhu Xi's assertion that "loving" (*qin* 親) is a corruption of the original text seems to reflect the increased interest in the phenomenon of "daily renewal" that was part of the Song social, political, and philosophical project going back to Hu Yuan. Overall, the *Daxue* provides a clear picture of the nested, isomorphic structures that mutually relate to and influence each other; and it brings us back to Zhu's insight that the crucial first step to achieving social peace and macrocosmic harmony begins at the microcosmic level of the well-tended heart-mind.

As Hon discusses, in drawing a connection between the *Daxue* and *Yijing*, Zhang Zai pays special attention to the 26th hexagram (*dachu* 大畜), translated variously as "The Taming Power of the Great," "The Great Nourisher," or, more literally, "Farming: Major."[42] A look at Zhang's work and the relevant source material gives some sense of what meaning-making via the *Yijing* looks like in practice. The corresponding statement on the 26th hexagram in the oldest layer of the *Yijing* is short and cryptic, and I rely here on Richard

Rutt's translation: "Favourable augury. Auspicious for eating away from home. Favourable for fording a big river."[43] Zhang Zai bases his own interpretation not on the hexagram statement but on one of the canonical commentaries that accompany it (in this case, *Tuan* 彖, or the first of the so-called Ten Wings). In Rutt's translation, the commentary reads:

> [The trigrams are] whole and "strong", solid and true, shining and bright, with daily renewal of powers. The whole line at the top honours men of worth. "Stopping" what is "strong" means firmly correcting. *Auspicious for eating away from home* means nurturing men of worth. *Favourable for crossing a big river*; (the 5th line) corresponds to (the 2nd line in) the Heaven trigram.[44]

With this, then, we turn to Zhang's own commentary on the commentary, as quoted by Hon:

> The *yang* trigram ascends and receives support from the *yang* line at the very top. Thus, [the *Tuan* statement says:] "Firmness and strength. Genuineness and Truth. Brilliance and light." Those engaging in moral cultivation often let their minds wander and spread themselves too thin on unimportant matters. [They do not know that] the best results come when their minds are focused .... In the *Yijing*, "*Gen*" stands for stopping. If one stops his mind from wandering, then he will be bright and clear .... If one is at rest, then he will be bright and clear. Thus the Great Learning speaks of one being able to reflect when he is at peace. If a person's mind wanders, he will not be bright and clear.[45]

Between the canonical commentary and Zhang's sub-commentary, we see many points covered in this chapter converging: the importance of a luminous and calm mind, the daily renewal of one's power, the belief that a practical program of moral self-cultivation is accessible to all, and the confidence that changes at the microcosmic level of the mind will palpably impact larger social, environmental, and cosmic structures.

Given the deep importance of the *Yijing* in Chinese culture, both in terms of scholarly study and popular divination practices, commentarial interventions in its accepted meaning will reverberate widely. New interpretations of its messages not only impact the understanding of the text but the understanding of all the other phenomena with which the text is correlated. Events in daily life will be interpreted differently, indeed, will be experienced differently—indeed will *be* different—because the ecology of interrelated correspondences that define what things "are" and "are not" has shifted. In this sense, *Yijing* textual exegetes are undoubtedly the creators of new values.

Realism and Realization

This last point brings us back to the question of what "creation" means in the *qi*-philosophical context. Numerous contemporary scholars have noted that Chinese philosophy in general lacks what in the West is called the "is–ought problem" or the distinction between values and facts.[46] According to this distinction, we have, on the one hand, what "is," or what simply exists, which we might describe as a scientist does, only observing what happens, when, and to what effect. On the other hand, we have what "ought to be," which we might describe as a moral philosopher does, looking for a rational basis to ground ethical deliberations. The problem, for the West, is that what "is" seems to have no necessary connection to what "ought to be." Here, we see again the interplay between familiar materialist, realist, and idealist positions: on one side, objectivity aligns with the bare existence of inert matter; on the other, subjectivity aligns with the inner life of the human mind; and the question becomes (yet again) whether or not our moral values are figments of our minds or "real" features of the objectively existing world.

Philosophers and scholars from Hu Yuan, to Zhang Zai, to Zhu Xi and many others would not ascribe to the fact–value distinction. The efficacious functioning of the cosmos is "good," just as the efficacious functioning of the human heart-mind is "good," and both senses of "good" have a moral valence. Or, as Hon comments, "As part of the ceaseless flow of *qi* in the universe, morality is understood metaphysically."[47] This has far-reaching implications for what we mean by the "creation" of new values. For one, the "creators" of values are not simply human agents. Chinese sources commonly refer to the functioning of the cosmos as the "heart-mind of the universe" (*tian di zhi xin* 天地之心), indicating a pervasive sentient aspect to all *qi*. For example, Zhu Xi says that even the smallest existing things have a degree of "heart-mind" (*xin* 心), though they may lack the characteristically human capacity for *zhijue*;[48] elsewhere he clarifies that the "heart-mind of the universe" does possess a sort of "numinous awareness" (*ling* 靈), which nonetheless differs from the "deliberative thought" (*silu* 思慮) of humans.[49] So, already we can clearly see that moral values need not be reduced to figments of the human mind.

Given this, we seem to be close to a realist position, in that moral values are indeed seen as real features of the existing cosmos. The contemporary analytic philosopher JeeLoo Liu echoes Hon in her discussion of a Ruist "moral metaphysics."[50] She uses the term "*qi*-realism" to capture the sense in which, as she says, *qi* "constitutes everything and is responsible for all changes."[51] This notion of *qi*-realism is insightful, so long as we understand it as adapting the realist position to a *qi*-based philosophy and not the other way around. Because, generally speaking, realism is driven by a different set of philosophical assumptions, and addresses itself to a different set of issues, than theories of *qi*. As we have seen, realism is usually taken to be a statement about the existence of things that are external to the human mind. The Chinese tradition certainly recognizes the dynamism of things around us, which may act in concord with us or resist us; but in a *qi*-based philosophy of correspondences and correlations, which is open to the rampant intermixing of *qi* in its various manifestations, it makes little sense to draw a hard line between inner and outer. This mismatch between realist theory and *qi*-philosophy becomes more pronounced if we consider the three common uses of realism within Western philosophy:

> (1) Realism in the contemporary analytic context is a theory about the language of truth claims and the referential structure of linguistic meaning, and it will be fairly uncontroversial to say that *qi*-philosophy is not engaging in that particular discourse.
>
> (2) More generally, realism in the sense of "naïve realism" purports to be the commonsense view that our senses give us reliable knowledge about what we perceive in the external world. The Chinese tradition, however, has deep suspicions about the reliability of the senses as well as the cogitations of the unsettled mind. In fact, accurate or appropriate understanding of the world around us requires years of practice and training—there is nothing "naïve" about the fully cultivated capacity for perception in the sense of *zhijue*.
>
> (3) Finally, realism has historically referred most frequently to metaphysical realism, going all the way back to interpretations of Plato's philosophy as a theory of the real existence of abstract universals. But *qi*-philosophy is not only, or even mostly, a metaphysical theory, although we may certainly derive metaphysical insights from it.[52] Rather, *qi*-philosophy is fundamentally a theory about the way things behave and, accordingly, a program for action.

Following from the final point, it seems that we should be talking not about "moral realism" here but "moral realization"—i.e., we are not making a comment about pre-given things, events, and values that are real, but we are engaging in techniques for realizing things, events, and values that are always only partly formed, partially given to us (and to each other), and partially created by us (and by each other). In the Chinese tradition, we are the meaningful products of a value-laden cosmos as much as we are the producers of values.

Listening to the Universe Speak

Following from that last point, Chinese traditions recognize the unique human capacity for not only participating in, but contributing to, the meaningful activities of the cosmos. As Hon says, for Zhang Zai, we humans

> assume the mission of sustaining the ceaseless flow of *qi* in the universe. Hence, he introduces the term "goodness" (*shan*) ... as a moral metaphysical category referring to one's wholehearted devotion to keeping the cosmic flow alive and refreshed. From the perspective of moral metaphysics, any mundane human affair—including the satisfaction of human biological needs such as food, drink, and sex—is vital to the human mission to continue the cosmic flow."[53]

We return, then, to the story of the two lovers at the start of the chapter, the one who heard the universe speaking to her, and the other who saw only the absurdity of contingency. As we quoted Milan Kundera, "it is right to chide man for being blind to such coincidences in his daily life. For he thereby deprives his life of a dimension of beauty."[54] I described this passage as having a lyrical significance—it is wistful to imagine that we beautify our lives by daring to take seriously the connections between mundane events, but it is also slightly sad, because we know it might only be our imagination, after all.

Some coincidences are certainly just coincidences, but Chinese philosophy at the outset takes seriously the significance of patterns, rhythms, repetitions, and correspondences. It begins by assuming the meaningfulness of existence itself, even in its most primal and inchoate state. Facticity, as the existentialist philosopher would call it, is not the dumb matter against which we hurl our human projects; but rather it is the dynamic and responsive *qi*-matrix, which possesses some degree of "numinous awareness," which is the wellspring of new values, and which is our co-creator in bringing such values forth.

That said, before we get too optimistic, the Chinese tradition certainly has its own occasions for waxing lyrical—the brevity of life, the inanity of political corruption, the folly of human ego—all of which contribute to its own set of existential worries. In the following chapter, we re-articulate the parameters of the existential condition from the perspective of the Buddhist, Ruist, and Daoist philosophies that we have so far investigated. Taking stock of the old existentialist values, we imagine new ones; responding to Nietzsche's call for a renewed health—"the *great health*"[55]—we look at practices for managing anxiety and solicitude (*you* 憂), enacting meaning through seriousness (*jing* 敬), manifesting the potency of stillness (*jing* 靜), attaining the creativity of sincerity (*cheng* 誠), and expressing the existential freedom of uncontrived spontaneity (*ziran* 自然).

4

Rituals for Existential Re-habituation

To speak, and to perform; this is ritual (言而履之，禮也).
Book of Rites (*Liji* 禮記)[1]

In a fascinating co-authored book *Ten Thousand Things: Nurturing Life in Contemporary Beijing,* Judith Farquhar and Zhang Qicheng use both philosophical and anthropological methods to engage the residents of Beijing in going about the everyday pursuit of the "good life." From healthy eating habits, to hobbies, to spiritual self-cultivation practices, these contemporary city-dwellers exemplify the values of "ceaseless renewal" (*shengsheng* 生生) and "ceaseless transformation" (*huahua* 花花) so important in *qi*-based philosophies. Farquhar and Zhang characterize their book as addressing the question of meaning in life, but they express some reservations about how the Western tradition frames that question:

> The problem with the question "What is the meaning of life" is with the question itself. The singularity of the copula "is" and the definite article "the" misleads in the direction of too much ambition. The question makes us suspect that there is something profound "out there" to be discovered …. If the insights of classical Chinese cosmogony at its most speculative are appreciated, and if traditional Chinese medicine both in theory and in practice is carefully read, existential and semantic questions about "meaning" become local, momentary, empirical. They become questions about the character, position, and form of some of the myriad things. Even philosophers reading this material find themselves

> inquiring not into ultimate truths, but into particular items of deep personal concern: the metaphysics of the Way turns attention to those sectors, regions, or collectivities of the myriad things that make up our actual lives.[2]

Their point is well taken and gives me cause to reflect on the general trajectory of the present book, because, for better or for worse, I am a product of Western existentialism, and my concern is indeed with ultimate questions.

What follows here is no doubt a highly speculative comparative exercise: working from key concepts in the European existential vocabulary, I explore corresponding terminology drawn from the range of East Asian discourses surveyed in the preceding two chapters. Certainly, none of the terms I select would be labeled as "existentialist" anywhere within these traditions themselves. In fact, taking the above passage from Farquhar and Zhang to heart, we can say that my own way of formulating existential questions is undoubtedly foreign to the *qi*-based worldview. As such, there will be a degree of mismatch: the terms I select are taken out of their indigenous intellectual history and used as a lens on the specific dilemmas of European existentialism. But I intend this mismatch to be productive—recalling the previous chapter's discussion of the term "realism" in JeeLoo Liu's phrase "*qi*-realism," my aim here is to adapt the existentialist position to *qi*-philosophy and not the other way around. In doing so, I seek not to answer my own existential questions as much as to gain new perspective on the habitual modes of thinking that sustain these lines of inquiry and consider possibilities for re-habituation.

In the main sections of this chapter, I work from a limited set of existential concepts important to the European discourse—namely, anxiety, absurdity, alienation, authenticity, and freedom—and replace each in turn with solicitude (*you* 憂), seriousness (*jing* 敬), stillness (*jing* 靜), sincerity (*cheng* 誠), and spontaneity (*ziran* 自然). All of the terms I consider are associated with one or more practices, be these scholarly methods, contemplative techniques, or closer to what Western discourses would call religious rituals. This is a crucial element in what I call above "re-habituation." As such, before we begin, some preliminary theoretical remarks are in order to orient our discussion of rituals and practices in a philosophical context.

Ritual Efficacy and Existential Transformation

Michel Foucault certainly was unaware of any affinity with the Song-dynasty Ruist scholarly tradition when he wrote the following: "I am not interested in the academic status of what I am doing because my problem is my own transformation .... This transformation of one's self by one's own knowledge is, I think, something rather close to the aesthetic experience."[3] Foucault was inspired not by Ruist views on studying and learning as methods of radical self-cultivation but instead by Pierre Hadot's work on the forgotten contemplative practices of ancient Greek and Roman philosophy. These ancient Western practices line up remarkably well alongside the pedagogies employed at Ruist academies from the Song and Ming periods. In Hadot's words, such "Stoico-Platonic inspired philosophical therapeutics" include research (*zetesis*), investigation (*skepsis*), reading (*anagnosis*), and meditation (*meletai*), which all contribute to the development of self-mastery (*enkrateia*) and the training of attention (*prosoche*), the latter of which Hadot identifies as "the fundamental Stoic spiritual attitude."[4] As he says:

> Attention to the present moment is, in a sense, the key to spiritual exercises. It frees us from the passions, which are always caused by the past or the future—two areas which do *not* depend on us. By encouraging concentration on the miniscule present moment, which, in its exiguity, is always bearable and controllable, attention increases our vigilance. Finally, attention to the present moment

allows us to accede to cosmic consciousness, by making us attentive to the infinite value of each instant, and causing us to accept each moment of existence from the viewpoint of the universal law of the *cosmos*.[5]

Through meditations that train the mind on the present moment, the Stoic philosopher learns to exert her will effectively over those circumstances under her control and to free herself from anxiety regarding those that are not. Such meditative practices include self-examination to identify our shortcomings, the use of memorization (*mneme*) to ingrain philosophical teachings into our minds, and imaginative reflections to help us appreciate the impermanence of material life from the larger perspective of the immaterial intellect.[6]

In a telling comment, for our purposes here, Hadot concludes his essay on "Spiritual Exercises" by saying, "Not until Nietzsche, Bergson, and existentialism does philosophy consciously return to being a concrete attitude, a way of life and of seeing the world."[7] Undoubtedly the attention to concrete, everyday experience is a key feature of existential philosophy, but I am hard-pressed to identify explicit instructions for "spiritual exercises" in the style of the ancient Stoics anywhere in existential writings.

On the one hand, we might consider Edmund Husserl's (1859–1938) method of epoché or "bracketing," or Henri Bergson's (1859–1941) method of intuition, both of which involve suspending our metaphysical assumptions so as to better attend to the qualities of immediate experience.[8] These phenomenological methods influenced the existential phenomenology of Heidegger in *Being and Time*, the hermeneutic strategies of Hans Georg Gadamer (1900–2002) in *Truth and Method*, and the non-dual account of experience in Maurice Merleau-Ponty's (1908–1961) *Phenomenology of Perception*. All such methods require cultivating a resistance to our own habitual modes of being that goes beyond just "critical thinking"—like Hadot says, the existentialists and phenomenologists present their methods as facilitating a fundamental reorientation toward a different way of life. But, apart from the basic intellectual insight needed to appreciate the methodologies, these philosophers do not speak of instructions for daily "spiritual exercises" like meditation, memorization, or imaginative visualization that might cultivate the capacity for the intellectual insight in question.

On the other hand, we might consider the more-or-less private lives of philosophers such as Bataille and Foucault, who did experiment (the former, notoriously[9]) with a range of Western practices aimed at altered states of consciousness, including various techniques of Christian mysticism. But, from the Stoics to the Neo-Platonists to Christian monastics, such practices are rooted in the very metaphysics of (spiritual) subject and (material) world that existential philosophy otherwise resists. One significant counterexample here might be Nietzsche's practice of hiking, his love of being in the mountains, and breathing mountain air. As Graham Parkes makes clear, Nietzsche's time spent in nature was a source not only of philosophical insight but also, we might say, philosophical vigor.[10] Like the Ruist meditator Gao Panlong we saw in the previous chapter, Nietzsche appreciated the invigorating effects that a solitary retreat in nature bestows on scholarly creativity. I am interested in contextualizing Nietzsche's hiking practice as part of a larger regimen. This is to say, I am interested in thinking through concrete exercises that better enact the values and non-dualist commitments of existentialism and thereby rethinking how we understand the term "practice" in a philosophical context.

If we turn our attention to Asian traditions, we see a gamut of practices—social norms, scholarly methods, rituals, rites, ceremonies, recitations, incantations, and so forth—that are not categorically distinguished from one another. For example, speaking of Buddhism in particular, T. Griffith Foulk comments: "Westerners interested in Zen ... are often attracted to the 'practices' of seated meditation (zazen), manual labor, and doctrinal study but uncomfortable with the 'rituals' of offerings, prayers, and prostrations made before images on altars."[11] But, he warns, "It is important to recognize that [these distinctions] are fundamentally alien to the East Asian Buddhist tradition of which Zen is a part. The East Asian Buddhist tradition itself has no words for discriminating what Westerners are apt to call 'ritual' as opposed to 'practice.'"[12]

Rather, these Asian traditions are home to a constellation of terms that might variously be translated as ritual, rite, practice, or training. These include: *li* (禮) or the Ruist rites, ceremonies, and social norms; *xing* (行), a term meaning actions, behaviors, or "doings," which is used in translating the Sanskrit *saṃskāra* (the conditioned habits that sustain delusion) and also *bhāvanā* (the liberating practices that cultivate enlightenment); and *xiu* (修), often referring to disciplined training or re-habituation.[13] Although contemporary compounds related to these terms do not map well onto the ritual–practice divide Foulk mentions, we do see a difference between formulaic rites performed only in certain contexts and pervasive ritualization that integrates organically into everyday life and, accordingly, a preference for achieving the latter.[14] And, moreover, this general tendency toward ritualized repetition as a technique for self- and social-transformation is common across Ruist, Buddhist, and Daoist traditions. For example, in a study of contemporary Japanese Rinzai Zen, Jørn Borup associates seemingly contrived Buddhist monastic protocols with "the Confucian concept of '*li*' ... meaning both social and moral conduct as well as religious ritual."[15] Similarly, Peter Yih-Jiun Wong speaks inclusively of the three major Chinese traditions when he describes the importance of rituals and practices across diverse strands of scholarship, even in cases of philosophical disagreement: "While Daoist criticisms of Confucianism are often directed at its preoccupation with matters ritualistic, nevertheless it shares with Confucianism a central concern: practice. That they disagree is precisely due to differing philosophical positions regarding it."[16] To capture this broad notion of ritual and practice that appears in all the East Asian traditions, Victor Hori uses the term "ritual formalism," which encompasses a cluster of words related to rites, practices, habits, and types of training or apprenticeship including "repetition, rote memorization, [and] behaving according to traditional prescription."[17] As he says, in both Buddhism and Ruism, "there is ... an educational use of ritual formalism: it trains consciousness."[18] Many activities we saw in the previous chapter—including practices of memorization and meditation employed in Ruist scholarly settings—would typify such "educational use."

This particular scholarly use of ritual is notably absent from Western philosophy, at least today.[19] As Kevin Schillbrack says, "There is at present a lack of philosophical interest in ritual. Philosophers (including philosophers of religion) almost never analyze ritual behavior; those who study ritual almost never refer to philosophy."[20] He credits the lack of philosophical interest in ritual to the general "assumption that ritual activities are thoughtless .... This assumption reflects a dichotomy between beliefs and practices and, ultimately, a general dualism between mind and body."[21] As for those who do study ritual, Schillbrack means mainly religious studies scholars, such as historians, anthropologists, or sociologists of religion. Researchers in these areas take a variety of approaches to issues of ritual and ritual efficacy, including studies of rituals as exchanges of social power, as psychologically therapeutic, or as types of so-called magical thinking.

One theoretical framework for understanding ritual efficacy, of particular interest to me here, relies on J. L. Austin's notion of performative utterances—that is, the idea that some words enact what they purport to accomplish through their very utterance, as saying the words "I promise" constitutes the promise itself, or uttering the vow

"I do" enacts the bond of marriage.[22] As Catherine Bell says, Austin's "simple insight that some words do things had a profound impact on studies of ritual."[23] Through performative enactment—swearing in presidents, creating sacred spaces, turning children into adults, and so forth—rituals manage the flow of social power that defines our shared world. Hence, scholars in religious studies may speak broadly about rituals as performative enactments of subjects *qua* subjects and the social relations that constitute them. Scholarship in this vein has been influenced by Foucault's notion of "technologies of self," already discussed, as well as Judith Butler's work on performativity, which was the first to consider Austin's language analysis in the context of Foucault's social constructivism.[24]

Via such theoretical turns, "ritual" becomes an inclusive category: it can refer specifically to liturgical rites and other religious activities, it can refer generally to social customs and cultural norms, and it can refer even more broadly to the very habits and performative enactments that constitute who we are. As the concept expands, the use of "ritual" in these more anthropological studies comes close to what philosophers Roger Ames and Henry Rosemont have called a "social grammar"[25] in their discussion of the term *li* (禮), referring to the ritual practices that shape selves and societies in the Chinese tradition.[26] Their point is underscored by their commitment to the process philosophy of A. N. Whitehead, which allows for the strong claim that actions constitute entities, or that the self "is," in concrete terms, what it "does." As they say in their introduction to the *Daodejing*, "It is only if the world is truly processive and changing in character that acquired dispositions may become a constitutive ground of the way things are."[27] Here, process philosophy speaks to the same critique of the metaphysical subject that drives phenomenology, existentialism, postmodernism, and social constructivism. Indeed, a processual worldview, whether Whiteheadian or Chinese, is well aligned with Jean-Paul Sartre's existentialist motto "existence precedes essence."[28]

At the level of theory, there are many compelling comparative points we might make regarding Austin, Foucault, Butler, Whitehead, existential philosophy, and Asian traditions.[29] But this brief overview of the role of ritual in philosophy and religious studies is meant here to help us identify and bracket our assumptions about what rituals are, what they "do," and whether they do anything "real" at all. My main concern is that various modernist and secular assumptions prepare us to take some ritual practices seriously and dismiss others as superstitious.[30] That is, we might understand Catholic communion as an exchange of social capital, or as a cathartic spiritual practice, but still dismiss the idea that wine "really" turns into blood as official Catholic doctrine maintains. The assumptions that underlie this dismissal need to be examined. In what follows, we will revisit an array of *qi*-based ritual practices while bracketing our assumptions, one way or another, about whether the efficacy of these practices can be explained in scientific, psychological, or sociological terms. As a result, in taking seriously a *qi*-based re-habituation of existentialist thought, we necessarily push back against existentialism's traditional resistance to metaphysical speculation.

Solicitude (*you* 憂) and Anxiety

We begin with a point of similarity: the Ruist tradition shares with existentialism a recognition of the basic disquietude that attends human life. For example, Heidegger distinguishes fear, which is object oriented, from anxiety, which is a pervasive sense of uncanny disorientation not attributable to any single frightening or threatening thing.[31] Unlike various real or imagined threats, anxiety does not fit meaningfully within the world as we know it or into any context where it makes sense. Hence death, or the possibility of our own utter nonexistence, is the quintessential trigger for anxiety in existentialist thought.

In Heidegger's terms, death "individuates" the person, which is to say, it calls her to face an experience that can always only be private, undisclosed.[32] As such, death marks a rupture in the social world of meaning—as that which is fundamentally my own, it can never be assimilated within any shared reality. For Heidegger, the confrontation with death marks both the end of one's uncritical acceptance of societal values and the beginning of the possibility of authentic personhood. This trajectory from anxiety to authenticity is related to Heidegger's central concept of "care" (*Sorge*), which he uses to refer to the fundamental "being" of the human being. The term signals our essential involvement in the lives that we find ourselves living, whether we are absorbed in the herd mentality driven by prevailing norms or awakened to authentic personhood through the encounter with death-anxiety. My questions for Heidegger concern not so much his theory of care and anxiety in *Being and Time* (which frankly I find compelling) but his lack of attention to the practices that enable any such existential awakening. He says that our conscience will "call" to us, but the call will be silent;[33] he says that our conscience will cause us to feel "guilty," not only for the inauthentic lives we have been leading but for even existing in the first place; he says that accepting this constitutive guilt will lead to authenticity.[34] What does any of this really mean?

The *Liji* (禮記) or *Book of Rites* offers insight into the connection between anxiety and care. It is a central text among the five Chinese classics, containing not only records of important early Ruist rites and ceremonies, but also philosophical reflections on the significance of ritual practice in human life. As Ames's and Rosemont's term "social grammar" suggests, the notion of "ritual" (*li* 禮) in Ruism casts a wide net, encompassing everything from dining etiquette, to state ceremonies, to procedures for worshipping at ancestral shrines. Accordingly, the efficacy of rituals is understood at multiple levels: some rituals are explicitly therapeutic, such as the mourning rites; others serve to disburse social capital by enforcing cultural and political hierarchies; while others seek to draw on (or conversely, ward off) the powers of unseen spirits and ghosts. In the most general sense, Ruist rituals include any formalized activities aimed at initiating, enhancing, or altering the productive alignment of microcosmic and macrocosmic structures in ourselves and in our world, and as such they can be understood within the same *qi*-based causal framework through which we have explained practices such as meditation, scholarly self-cultivation, and *Yijing* divination.

On the topic of anxiety, the *Liji* tells us that a sense of "solicitude" always accompanies self-cultivation: "The exemplary person [*junzi* 君子] experiences a lifetime of solicitude [*you* 憂] but not a moment of worry [*huan* 患]."[35] The term *you* (憂) can mean to be anxious, concerned, or mournful, and also to be weighed down by care or deep sympathy. In English, "solicitude" expresses both of these aspects of anxiousness and caring concern. The important distinction for the text is between solicitude and the near-synonymous term "worry" (*huan* 患). Contemporary scholar Michael Ing suggests that *huan* refers to worries that arise over our own personal failings, resulting from inadequate effort on our own parts, such as a lack of self-discipline or a failure to fulfill our obligations. In contrast, he says, *you* refers to anxiety arising from a more fundamental vulnerability or, we might say, existential uncertainty.[36] Even the most disciplined and well-prepared person is still vulnerable to the unforeseen vicissitudes of life. Unlike the Stoic philosophers, who would have us believe that we should make peace with circumstances that are beyond our control, the *Liji* seems to consign us to a lifetime of watchful anxiety.

The *Liji*'s message is complicated by the fact that Kongzi (孔子, i.e., Confucius) says various contradictory things about *you* throughout the *Analects* (*Lunyu* 論語). Some of his comments seem to directly oppose the *Liji*, as in 9.29: "Those that are wise are not confused, those that are humane are not solicitous [*you* 憂], and those that are brave are not fearful [*ju* 懼]."[37] Elsewhere, however, in 14.28, he explicitly places this level of attainment beyond of the reach of most people: "The way of the exemplary person [*junzi* 君子] is threefold, but it is beyond my reach: to be humane and not solicitous; wise and not confused; brave and not fearful."[38] And, finally, in 7.3, Kongzi discusses his own solicitous anxieties: "That I have not cultivated my moral power, that I have not explained what I have learned, that I have not aligned with what I know to be appropriate, and that I have been unable to change what is not good—these are what cause my solicitude."[39] Here, for Kongzi at least, the line between his personal failings and larger existential uncertainties remains ambiguous.

For this very reason, speculates Ing, Kongzi appears as an exemplary but relatable figure in Chinese traditions: "Confucius, in this sense, is fully human and stands in for us as we stand in for him."[40] Speaking more generally, Ing suggests that the Ruist tradition encourages us to manage our anxieties so that they contribute to what he calls "productive disorientations," which arise when there is a mismatch between the way we expect the world to work and the way events actually unfold: "The Confucian project sets out to order the world; yet the anxiety associated with this project's contingency on governmental structures beyond the control of Confucians is never fully resolved."[41] This is, we might say, the basic "existential anxiety" of the Ruist worldview—that even our best efforts cannot sway the tide of impending disorder, that the cosmos is not especially receptive to our interventions, and above all that our moral exemplars are as ineffective as the rest of us.

This disorientation is "productive," in Ing's sense, because it drives us to re-engage with circumstances that seem out of hand and to develop new strategies for establishing order. As he says, the *Liji* traces the origin of ritual itself to the overwhelming disorientation of human mortality and bodily vulnerability. For example, he quotes the following passage from the "Liyun" (禮運) chapter: "Ritual originated ... when someone died. [The living] climbed up to the rooftop and called [after them] saying: 'Alas! You [must] come back!'"[42] This is the *Liji*'s own explanation for why the traditional mourning rites require family members to climb to the roofs of their homes and call out for the deceased. The ritual works in accord with our own heartfelt tendencies, while channeling our emotions and helping us to manage their overwhelming force.

Elsewhere, in *Analects* 2.6, a student asks Kongzi about the meaning of "filial piety" or "family reverence" (*xiao* 孝), which refers to the hierarchical familial relations central to the proper performance of a multitude of Ruist rites. Regarding the meaning of *xiao*, Kongzi answers: "The solicitous anxiety of parents regarding their children's health" (父母唯其疾之憂).[43] The cryptic passage has been rendered variously in English as "Parents are anxious lest their children should be sick" (James Legge) and "Give your mother and father nothing to worry about beyond your physical well-being" (Ames and Rosemont).[44] Either way, the passage underscores Ing's basic point that ritualized actions are deeply related to fundamental human anxieties:

> A central theme [in the *Liji*] is that human beings naturally have feelings that well up within themselves as a result of encountering certain circumstances in life. Without ritual, these feelings will be directionless. They will manifest themselves in random—and likely destructive—actions.... Rituals are the tools for providing direction and cultivating a habituated sense of proper performance.[45]

All in all, Ing helps us to think of rituals as what we might call existential coping strategies. They make use of preexisting tendencies—in this case, our raw emotions—while shaping and developing our capacity to endure otherwise overwhelming anxieties.

In a more speculative vein, we can make a similar point regarding cosmic tendencies and ritual transformations. Following the speculative developments of the Song dynasty, we find an increased focus on the ability of humans to engage with and influence larger cosmic patterns via the pursuit of efficacious correspondences. As discussed in the previous chapter, certain structural tendencies (*li* 理) are evident in the behavior of *qi*, beginning with the polarity of *yin* and *yang* and extending to the increasingly complex orders of meaning that arise from the recursive interactions of matter-energy across macrocosmic and microcosmic levels. By using ritualized behaviors (*li* 禮) to align with and exploit these tendencies, humans can influence transformations in the world that go beyond the psychological (as in the mourning rites that help us deal with grief) or the sociological (as in the protocols of family etiquette that maintain harmonious relations).

The solicitous anxiety that attends the Ruist worldview concerns whether ritual efficacy in fact dramatically diminishes the farther out we attempt to go, reflecting a cosmos that is not especially attentive to human well-being. But, very much in line with the liberatory potential of anxiety in Heidegger's work, this solicitude can also be productive and drive us toward renewed engagement. The "productive disorientation" that Ing discusses, like Heidegger's death-anxiety, causes ruptures in our everyday world, where what we thought we knew is called into question and thereby new understanding becomes possible. It is not so much the mysterious "call of conscience" but specific instances of trying and failing to realize the meaning we seek that draws our attention to our own desires, dissatisfactions, capacities, and limitations. When facing these points of congruence and tension between microcosmic and macrocosmic structures, a *qi*-based philosophy points a way forward with reference to concrete techniques, including ritual and, as discussed next, the intentional cultivation of "seriousness" (*jing* 敬).

Seriousness (*jing* 敬) and Absurdity

As Ing notes above, rituals require us to cultivate "a habituated sense of proper performance," indicating that part of their efficacy lies in our manner of conducting them. According to Ruist terminology, we are to carry out ritual with an air of "reverence" or "seriousness" (*jing* 敬). This is often described as adopting a respectful demeanor and maintaining a sense of watchful apprehensiveness in all matters, whether alone or in public. Zhu Xi identifies seriousness as a central technique for self-cultivation that assures proper alignment between the heart-mind and larger macrocosmic structures.[46] As such, it accomplishes the performative enactment at the heart of ritual's effectiveness.

Philosopher Stephen C. Angle identifies *jing* as the practice most deserving of renewed attention if we are interested in establishing the relevance of Song and Ming thought for contemporary moral and political theory. *Jing* is directed toward the enactment of the central Ruist values of harmony (*he* 和) and structure (*li* 理, rendered in Angle's translation as "coherence"). Both are to be understood as ongoing processes that must be constantly renegotiated and reestablished, nurtured and cultivated, in ways that promote mutual flourishing across the microcosmic and macrocosmic levels of existence.[47] Angle describes *jing* as the feeling of "awe" that one might experience before the vast yet intimate interconnectedness of the cosmos,[48] as well as specific techniques for "posture, expression, and behavior" needed to efficaciously promote cosmic coherence and harmony via ritual enactments.[49]

Here, the Ruist value of *jing* seems very different from the existential notion of absurdity, which expresses the fear that all matters we take seriously are ultimately trivial.[50] In a world of absurdity, our actions are, in the words of Milan Kundera, "as free as they are insignificant."⁵¹ In contrast, he says, a serious world is one grounded in the certainty of purposeful creation: "Behind all the European faiths, religious and political, we find the first chapter of Genesis, which tells us that the world was created properly, that human existence is good, and that we are therefore entitled to multiply."⁵² The Ruist tradition has its own debates with Daoism over the issue of life's absurdity, but their disagreement does not hinge on the presence or absence of a purposeful creator. Thus, the Ruist notion of *jing* or "seriousness" gives us an alternative perspective on the nature and scope of absurdity.

The early Daoist texts are famed for making light of supposedly serious human concerns. Throughout the *Daodejing* (道德經) and the *Zhuangzi* (莊子), Ruists are satirized for their fastidious adherence to ritual norms and their pedantic squabbling over textual exegesis. Chapter eighteen of the *Daodejing* summarily rejects the laundry list of Ruist moral values—humaneness (*ren* 仁), wisdom (*zhi* 知), righteousness (*yi* 義), and family reverence (*xiao* 孝)— as misguided contrivances.⁵³ The fifth chapter goes even further, declaring that the cosmos itself is "inhumane" (*buren* 不仁) and treats us all as if we were disposable.⁵⁴ Finally, it would be difficult to miss the air of resignation expressed in chapter twenty: "All this nonsense! Does it ever come to an end? Most people are happy-happy, as though feasting at a banquet, or climbing some sightseeing tower in the spring. I alone am impassive, revealing nothing, like a baby that has yet to smile; listless, nowhere to go."⁵⁵ Despite these passages, it would be a mistake to read European nihilism back into the *Daodejing*. The cosmos may be indifferent, and human conventions may be silly contrivances, but existence is not absurd— the *dao* follows its own course, in its own time, and fosters its own meaningful order: "It gives life to things and nurtures them. Giving life without possessing, acting without demanding reward, raising things without lording it over them—this is called the profoundest power [*de*]."⁵⁶ As translators Roger Ames and David Hall point out, in their comment on this passage, there is certainly no purposeful creator in the Daoist picture, and yet the text seems to marvel at the dazzling variety of existence, not despair over its absurdity: "The dynamic field of experience is the locus in which the stream of phenomena is animated and achieves consummation, but all of this pageantry occurs without the presence of some controlling hand. The energy of transformation lies within the process itself rather than in some external agency. It is the very nature of the world to transform."⁵⁷

As said in the previous chapter, the surrounding world into which we are born is not the resistant field of mute objects described in existentialism as "facticity" but the responsive matter–energy matrix of *qi*. Even its most basic interactions—such as the originary division into *yin* and *yang* polarity—is meaning-generating, which is to say that the very distinction of *yin* and *yang* is a value-laden distinction. From there, all further interactions of increasing complexity only add to the rampant proliferation of value, resulting in the world as we know it. Speaking as broadly as possible, we can say that *to be* at all is *to be meaningfully* in this "moral metaphysics."⁵⁸

With this in mind, another way to frame the existential anxiety of the Ruist worldview, mentioned above, would be to say that Ruists worry not so much over whether life is meaningful but over the place of human beings within a value-laden universe. Are human concerns more or less dwarfed by the awesomeness of cosmic meaning-making, as the Daoists seem prone to believe? Or do humans in fact play a special role in conducting the great orchestra of meaning that surrounds us? Either way, absurdity is not an option—our actions, to return to Kundera's phrase, are never "as free as they are insignificant." To the contrary, our every action is weighed down by consequences that reverberate throughout the matter–energy matrix, affecting ourselves and others. Seriousness is precisely the practice through which we align our minds with the *gravity* of the present moment, and my use of "gravity" here is intentional: the weight of our value-laden existence is as palpable as the so-called laws of physics that shape our universe, where both moral values and physical forces speak to structural tendencies of *qi* that are not categorically different from each other.

So, reviewing what we have so far, ritual (*li* 禮) is a way to address existential vulnerability by ordering our actions to account for their inescapable efficacy, or a way to rein in, as it were, the possibility of unforeseen consequences; and seriousness (*jing* 敬), the manner in which we conduct ritual, is a way to align the mind and thereby attune ourselves to the gravity of our microcosmic–macrocosmic interconnectedness in every given moment. Seriousness marks a sharp turn away from any sense of absurdity, as this is expressed in European existentialism, but it does not thereby overcome the solicitude (*you* 憂) that can and should beset us, given the weight of our existential condition. Next we turn to a set of related practices, also aimed at attuning the heart-mind, but which focus on contemplative or meditative techniques, and which, in this sense, do offer strategies for managing the solicitous anxieties that we unavoidably face.

Stillness (*jing* 靜) and Alienation

In existential thought, the individuating force of death-anxiety and the demoralizing effect of absurdity can contribute to a sense of "alienation," or the solipsistic estrangement from one's own self, other people, and the surrounding world. Sartre deals with alienation throughout *Being and Nothingness* in his exploration of the question of how the subject gains access to anything outside of its own awareness. Ultimately, his solution hinges on the idea of non-being. Objective reality in general is described as a plenum or "full positivity" in Sartre's terms, which in itself seems to be undifferentiated; it is only via the thinking subject that nothingness or non-being is used to distinguish one thing from another, which is to say, one thing from what it is not. In Sartre's own terminology, he says: "There must exist a Being (this cannot be the In-itself) of which the property is to nihilate Nothingness, to support it in its being, to sustain it perpetually in its very existence, *a being by which nothingness comes to things*."[59] Despite Sartre's comments about the full positivity of being in itself, it remains unclear whether the deployment of nothingness reflects some special power of the subject or is a feature of reality in general.[60]

Fiona Ellis compellingly argues that Sartre remains committed to the basic realist position that individual things are not simply figments of our minds. As she says, Sartre seems to uphold a distinction between the mechanistic causal relations that characterize objective reality and the freedom of the thinking subject, whose capacity to conceptualize things is not simply an effect of the presence of things themselves.[61] In other words, he does not deny the existence of things outside the mind, but he rejects the claim that these external things simply determine what we know and perceive. We quote Ellis's argument in full, as it serves as a bridge to our discussion of stillness (*jing* 靜) as an existential value:

> The difficulty ... centres on the question of how best to understand Sartre's claim that non-being is a feature of reality whilst also accommodating his idea that it originates in consciousness. The idea that non-being is a feature of reality fits well with the idea that it brings distinction to things, yet this latter interpretation, when linked to the claim that non-being originates in consciousness, seems to accord a constructive role to consciousness. By contrast, if we abandoned this constructive conception of consciousness whilst also retaining the idea that non-being is in the world, it is

difficult to see how non-being can originate in us so as to figure in an explanation of how we gain access to things. Our investigation of Sartre's view of the relation between the conceptual realm and the causal order promised to break this dilemma, for it made clear the sense in which non-being is intended to account for our capacity to conceptualise a ready-made world of things. Thus, it is possible to allow that non-being originates in us whilst avoiding the conclusion that the mind's work is to be viewed in constructive terms.

Two comparative points can be made. Firstly, the Chinese tradition can accommodate one part of the puzzle that seems to stump both Sartre and Ellis, namely, that there is a correspondence between the capacities of the mind and the tendencies of things in the world. In other words, a lingering question at the end of Ellis's argument is why our minds would have this "capacity to conceptualize" that, seemingly inexplicably, lines up with the "ready-made world of things." As we have seen, a *qi*-based philosophy premises itself on the existence of precisely such correspondences. Secondly, the Chinese tradition is not at all resistant to the suggestion that "the mind's work is to be viewed in constructive terms." Indeed, as we saw in the previous chapter, the mind's capacity to relax into a state of stillness is the source of its radically constructive powers.

Sartre's claim about the role of nothingness or non-being in differentiating things is largely an epistemological point. Turning to a *qi*-based philosophy, we should speak not of nothingness but of the formless or inchoate *qi* that allows for the emergence of new forms; and, with that, we are making less an epistemological point and more an ontological one. To review, we have already seen several strategies for relaxing the mind into the state of stillness that draws on the creative power of formless *qi*. Firstly, Kim Iryŏp's conception of meditation seems to reflect a *qi*-based understanding of Buddhist emptiness as an energy that emanates from the mind of the meditator, with the power to disrupt the normal causal order of the karmically determined world. Secondly, Ruist quiet-sitting practices, meant to prepare the mind for learning, allow the mind to draw on the primordial raw material of unformed *qi*, enabling its capacity to manifest new forms and new orders of harmony or coherence. And thirdly, these practices can be further related to Daoist meditations such as "sitting and forgetting" (*zuowang* 坐忘) and "fasting the heart-mind" (*xinzhai* 心齋), all of which are believed to have a healthy and reinvigorating effect on the mind and body.

In all cases, the efficacious emanation of mental energy in the world, which is undoubtedly creative and constructive, is enabled only through the daily renewal of the mind's power to manifest forms, which is what a meditation practice confers. Hence, although alienation may be a problem for petty people (*xiaoren* 小人), whose heart-minds remain limited and agitated, such alienation can be overcome via meditative techniques for relaxing the mind into its formless and expansive state. This is why stillness and the meditative practices that cultivate it are key terms in this cross-cultural existential study.

So far, we have looked at three techniques for self-cultivation that are ritualistic and contemplative to varying degrees: (1) the diligent practice of social rituals, which help align humans to each other and to their shared world, and which respond directly to the fundamental existential vulnerabilities of the Chinese philosophical worldview; (2) the regular maintenance of seriousness, which, as a technique for regulating the heart-mind, aids in the efficacious ritual enactment of meaning; (3) the daily renewal of mental powers via the cultivation of stillness, which employs meditative or contemplative methods, and which relates to the efficacious manifestation of thought in the world. The last point reminds us of the key claim appearing in both Chapters 2 and 3, namely, that mental energies do not remain confined within the body in this cross-cultural existential framework we are constructing. Next, we turn to two final terms, associated with the techniques above, which together help to chart the trans-egoic scope of value creation in the East Asian context. Below, sincerity (*cheng* 誠) and spontaneity (*ziran* 自然) stand in for the existentialist themes of authenticity and freedom, concluding this small set of *qi*-based existential terms with a focus on the ideals that guide practice.

Sincerity (*cheng* 誠) and Authenticity

The philosophers Roger Ames and David Hall will perhaps forever live in infamy, at least in some sinological circles, because they chose to translate *cheng* (誠) as "creativity." By far, the more common English translations are "sincerity" or "integrity." Without taking a stance on their contentious word choice, I am nonetheless interested in the reasoning behind their decision, which helps to articulate precisely the connection between *cheng* and the creation of new values that I take as central in this catalogue of *qi*-based existential terminology.

Ames and Hall begin with a general comment on the nature of creativity: "Either everything shares in creativity, or the world is sharply divided into *creators* and *created*—that is, *makers* and *made*."[62] A *qi*-based philosophy, as they say, gives us a world of "ontological parity" where creativity is always "transactional and multi-dimensional,"[63] and therefore self-cultivation can be seen as a co-creative activity involving selves, societies, and whole environments.[64] Following this, they conclude that sincerity and integrity must be understood holistically not as subjective states but as developmental processes that encompass and unite multiple agencies and energies. In their own words, "The dynamic of becoming whole, construed aesthetically, is precisely what is meant by a creative process. It is thus that *cheng* is to be understood as creativity."[65] For my part, I will continue to use the more common English term "sincerity" in what follows, albeit in a dynamic and processual sense, because I wish to highlight connections between this usage of sincerity and the existentialist notion of "authenticity."[66]

Authenticity cannot help but be a contested value in existential philosophy, given the overall resistance to speculative metaphysics. In other words, existentialists cannot take authenticity to mean "being true to oneself," if this implies fidelity to a metaphysically "real" subject; nor can it mean being true to one's highest ideals, if this implies conformity to a pre-given set of moral facts. The English word "authenticity" is used to translate Martin Heidegger's neologism *Eigentlichkeit*, meaning something like "own-ness," or "owned-ness," or one's "ownmost."[67] For Heidegger, a person first encounters herself while in the midst of living a life she did not choose, going along with the flow of societal norms and values, with little thought as to whether or why any of it matters.[68] She only stops to question the meaning of her existence when she confronts the thought of her own mortality, resulting in the anxious individuation, as described above, that first makes authentic personhood possible. Not surprisingly, Heidegger spends more time talking about the death-anxiety that provokes the break with the social world and less time describing any practices associated with authenticity.

In other existentialist work, such as that of Simone de Beauvoir, the question of authenticity is related to the conflict between freedom and facticity—the freedom of the subject unconstrained by any pre-given metaphysical essence determining who or what it is, in contrast with the facticity of the embodied and socially conditioned state of being into which it has been born.[69] There is an echo here of the Stoic distinction between what falls under my control and what does not, in that authentic existence must involve coming to terms with what I cannot control while nonetheless fully embracing my life choices as my own. Although both Beauvoir and Sartre discuss concrete existential dilemmas and relate their theories to everyday situations (jobs, love affairs, political causes), they, like Heidegger, do not provide much in the way of practical instruction for cultivating authenticity.

The notion of *cheng*, in contrast, is closely associated with several Ruist practices. We earlier encountered it in the previous chapter at a critical juncture in the *Daxue* or "Great Learning." As we learned from that text, the investigation of things (*gewu* 格物) and the extension of knowledge (*zhizhi* 致知) allow thoughts or intentions (*yi* 意) to become sincere (*cheng* 誠). Following this crucial step, the mind becomes correct, the self is cultivated, the household regulated, the state well-ordered, and the whole world brought to peace.[70] Our first clue, then, to what *cheng* means in the Ruist context lies in the two practices that enable its development: investigating things and extending knowledge.

In Ruism, the term "investigating things" can connote empirical observation (especially astronomical study), but it most often refers to reading the classical texts, commentaries, and various histories to gain a sense of the structural tendencies (*li* 理) that characterize humans and their worlds. In the words of Kong Yingda (574–648), author of an influential *Daxue* commentary, the person who aims at *cheng* must begin with "studying and learning" (*xuexi* 學習).[71] In a later commentary, Zhu Xi associates studying and learning with "extending knowledge" and the desire (*yu* 欲) to make one's knowledge inexhaustible (*wubujin* 無不盡).[72] I understand this in conjunction with his comment, in the same section, that thoughts or intentions (*yi* 意) are what the mind "emits" or sends forth (*fa* 發),[73] as well as with his comments elsewhere that the extension of knowledge means to "enter into things."[74] Both ideas underscore our recurring theme that the psychical energies of human thoughts and emotions can, at times, extend beyond the borders of the body. In fact, Zhu notes that "human *qi* and the *qi* of the cosmos are constantly interacting,"⁷⁵ but of course we are not always in tune with these energetic flows or capable of managing them efficaciously. This is why, as Joseph Adler comments, in Zhu Xi's thought "there is a moral imperative for learning, and the process of learning is a psycho-spiritual transformation that refines and clarifies one's *qi*."⁷⁶ Adler goes on to make explicit the connections between educational techniques for refining *qi* and attaining sage-like sincerity: "In human beings, spirit [*shen* 神] is a quality of mind—specifically mind-*qi* in its finest, most free-flowing state .... To embody this epistemological potential ... is to be a fully authentic (*cheng*) human being, a Sage."⁷⁷

The extension of knowledge, then, in Zhu Xi's sense of "emitting thought" and "entering into things," refers not only to the scope of what I understand but also to the efficacy of the mental energy that I put out into the world. When knowledge is efficacious in this way, then the emanations of the mind are "sincere," in that microcosmic thoughts and feelings and surrounding macrocosmic circumstances are efficaciously attuned to each other. This all serves to show why the English term "sincerity" is strained when used to translate *cheng* and sheds further light on Ames's and Hall's choice of "creativity" instead. In other words, in common English usage, sincerity connotes truthfulness or genuineness, which would seem to imply that a person's words, attitudes, and feelings conform to a pre-given set of objective facts about the world; in contrast, for Zhu Xi, *cheng* refers to the potency of cultivated mental energies that, when properly aligned, aid in bringing about well-ordered people, families, and societies. *Cheng* is precisely the enactment—the making real or making true—of new order in the world.

The text most closely associated with the study of *cheng*, the *Zhongyong*, expresses this notion of creativity as a process of world-enactment:

> In the world only someone of perfect *cheng* 誠 is considered able to complete his nature. Someone who is able to complete his nature is then able to complete the natures of others. Someone who is able to complete the natures of others is then able to complete the natures of things. Someone who is able to complete the natures of things is then able to assist Heaven and Earth in their transforming [*hua* 化] and creating [*yu* 育]. Someone who can assist Heaven and Earth in their transforming and creating can then join with Heaven and Earth as a triad.[78]

Echoing Kim Iryŏp's notion of enlightened beings as creators of culture, here the person of perfect *cheng* is a co-creator of worlds, manifesting or realizing shared value in conjunction with the forces of the cosmos. In the Ruist commentary of Zheng Xuan (127–200), he defines "completing nature" (*jinxing* 盡性) in this passage as "following *li*" (*shunli* 順理), or acting in accord with the structural tendencies by which *qi* manifests the myriad forms of life as we know it. Note, these forms are not predetermined, and their success is not guaranteed. Zheng says that the person who follows *li* can help prevent things from losing their coherence or integrity, or literally, their "whatness," as in Ian Johnston's and Wang Ping's translation: "'Completing nature' refers to [things] following principle, causing them not to lose their 'whatness'" (盡性者，謂順理之使不失其所也).[79] The phrase might also be translated as "causing them not to lose their place." In this sense, the comment connotes both the internal coherence by which one thing comes to be what it is and the external coherence by which it comes to fit within a larger context.

This is all to say that *cheng* can be glossed as sincerity not in the sense of being true to a pre-given reality but in the sense of making true or bringing forth an as-yet-unrealized world. In the words of the *Zhongyong*, such sincere action will "combine" or "unify" (*he* 合) the internal and external aspects of *dao* (*wai nei zhi dao* 外內之道), thereby ensuring integrity.[80] This is a key point—integrity is an achievement reflecting a process of integration, bringing together the internal and external; it does not bring the subject in line with a pre-given reality but manifests a reality in which both selves and worlds, microcosms and macrocosms, are reoriented to each other. For this same reason, *cheng* is described as "ceaseless" (*wuxi* 無息),[81] indicating the need for constant reintegration to accommodate the ever-shifting terrain always emerging anew from the combined efforts of humans, environmental forces, and cosmic powers.

As mentioned earlier, Sartre's existentialist dictum that "existence precedes essence" seems to accord with the processual worldview expressed by the *Daxue* and *Zhongyong*; but, I venture to guess, the overall resistance to speculative metaphysics in existential thought would preclude Sartre, Beauvoir, and others from linking their ideas to a *qi*-based philosophy. Hence, European existentialism lacks the explanatory framework to conceive of authenticity as the process of world-enactment that *cheng* conveys. Such beliefs about the transegoic powers of the mind underscore what we described in the previous chapter as the "non-naïve" aspects of existential speculation, or the sense in which existential anxieties over absurdity and alienation can be addressed via techniques that develop the mind's powers beyond the limited inner awareness of solipsistic subjectivity.

Spontaneity (*ziran* 自然) and Freedom

As a cultivated achievement, *cheng* arises through diligent ritualistic and contemplative practices, including the Ruist rites, the cultivation of mental seriousness and stillness, and, as we have seen above, the intentional use of reading and learning as daily activities that sustain human meaning-making. The idea that uncontrived sincerity is made possible only via purposeful training is also reflected in the term *ziran* (自然), which literally means "self-so," and which has been translated as naturalness, spontaneity, or that which happens of its own accord. The term appears in descriptions of how primordial *qi* spontaneously manifests *yin* and *yang*, how the mind spontaneously reverts to its expansive and formless state during meditative practices, and also how diligent training can enable seemingly uncontrived improvisational virtuosity. Several well-known stories in the early Daoist text *Zhuangzi* praise individuals who attain superhuman skills after a lifetime of focused training—for example, there is cook Ding who, after years of practice, can cut up an ox without ever dulling his blade; or the man with a severely bent spine, who gains the admiration of Kongzi after having practiced for months to perfect the skill of flawlessly catching cicadas.[82] The text explains that what accounts for such astonishing skill is the ability to forget oneself and one's learning. We see this in the nineteenth chapter, where a carpenter carves an exquisite bell-stand after fasting for seven days so as to forget himself entirely, and the artist Shui can make perfect circles and squares because his hands move like a force of nature, without allowing his intellect to get in the way.[83]

Anyone familiar with artistic or musical improvisation will understand this connection between practice, forgetting, and spontaneous creation, and this dynamic is frequently referenced in East Asian approaches to teaching and learning. As linguist Masako K. Hiraga points out, in an article on contemporary Japanese pedagogy, tea ceremony students cultivate their skills through diligent imitation, which eventually leads to improvisational creativity:

> The students just observe how the master (or the instructor assigned by the master) serves tea, and imitate it, repeat it, practice it, until the master says that they have passed the test to become a junior master. The students (junior masters) are then allowed to transform or manipulate the model they have acquired and internalized, in order to become a senior master, who can now leave the world of the former master to create one's own style and model. This course

of development is called 守 *syu* [*shu*], 破 *ha*, 離 *ri* ('keep, break, and leave') in traditional Japanese arts.[84]

Students of Japanese martial arts also follow this dictate "keep, break, leave," in which the first stage focuses on learning set forms or *kata* through repetition, and the last stage focuses on leaving the forms behind to enable spontaneous improvisation. Such improvised "spontaneity" marks not a break with tradition but a development of the tradition itself. In other words, the practitioner at the last stage is not a solo agent simply making up new moves; rather, he or she is an extension of the tradition and, in turn, extends the tradition into new territory.

Building on our discussion of commentarial writing in the third chapter, we turn to the concept of *ziran* here to rethink the meaning of creativity and freedom in an existential context. As we said in relation to *Yijing* commentary and political activism, new values arise through the skillful subversion of the old, which is not an outright rejection of the past. Quite to the contrary, such skillful subversion maintains a sense of reverential connection to the past and derives part of its power precisely from this continuity. Subversive creation avoids, above all, direct confrontation between competing values or conflicts between competing wills. Both Buddhist and Daoist discourses express the idea of *ziran* via a cluster of terms related to indirect action, which can be translated literally as "no-action" (*wuwei* 無為), "no-thought" (*wunian* 無念), and so forth. Bradley Park captures the sense in which indirect action is effective precisely to the extent that the agent is not limited by her own ego or petty self:

> *Wuwei* is precisely an attempt to capture the experiential sense of an activity developing spontaneously (*ziran*, 自然), rather than on the basis of the subject's spontaneity, qua "doing" (*wei*, 為). In other words, one is notably conscious of the absence of egocentered initiative and control in the case of skill-in-action. To consciously

assert agency in the midst of skillful flow is to puncture the continuity of its unfolding and deflate the quality of the performance—to try and seize the experience of flow is to lose it.[85]

Comparative philosophers have disagreed over whether Nietzsche's notion of the will to power, which underlies his views on the creation of new values, can be compared to Buddhist to Daoist ideas of non-egoic action as described by Park above.[86] Rather than enter into to these disagreements myself, I only point out here—as I have maintained throughout this book—that we must look outside Nietzsche's own writings if we seek advice on specific practices that might develop our powers, non-egoic or otherwise (with the exception, of course, as mentioned above, of Nietzsche's avid hiking practice).

Understanding our existential freedom and creativity on the model of *ziran*, we gain an important insight: the training that enables freedom is not necessarily directed at what the individual wants to do or create, but rather at curbing the ego and expanding consciousness so as to facilitate the spontaneous arising of value and meaning. Such value is not the product of a solo agent but instead emerges in a shared environmental context, taking us back to Kim Iryŏp's idea that meditators are creators of whole cultures or the *Zhongyong*'s idea that sincerity is a kind of world-enactment. As has been evident across all the Buddhist, Daoist, and Ruist sources we have studied so far, these instances of creativity refer to trans-egoic practices that are especially powerful precisely to the extent that they operate indirectly and spontaneously.

The Radical Existentialism of Ruist Thought

The above notion of spontaneity may be most often attributed to Daoism, but as Stephen C. Angle discusses at length, naturalness and spontaneity are key features of "sagely ease" in Ruist thought as well.[87]

Given that, we can appreciate that all of the terms above are Ruist by association, meaning that we have traveled from the radical politics of a twentieth-century Buddhist nun and feminist activist to a relatively traditional set of Ruist values. What are we to make of this trajectory?

Fully understanding Kim Iryŏp's existential vision took us from her Buddhist practice in the context of a karmic economy to her views on "life-energy" against the backdrop of *yin-yang* cosmology and *qi*-philosophy. At this point, I suggest that her commitment to meditation as itself a form of political activism—as an activity fundamentally oriented toward enacting a better social order— underscores the Ruist sensibilities in her thinking. On the one hand, this is counterintuitive, given that her feminism was very much a product of anti-Ruist sentiments associated with a number of modernizing movements across East Asia in her lifetime.[88] On the other hand, very little of Buddhism in East Asia can be understood apart from the broader Ruist cultural context and long-standing beliefs about the mutual compatibility of the three dominant traditions of Ruism, Daoism, and Buddhism. When Buddhism first arrived in China, it was the subject of various critiques—monasticism in particular was seen as undermining people's natural loyalties to their family and government; the Buddhist philosophical account of emptiness was seen as promoting nihilism and moral relativism; and various ritual practices were accused of courting unsavory spiritual forces.[89] In response, Buddhists slowly accommodated themselves to the Ruist political and social context, often by stressing the many ways that Buddhist institutions function in the service of family and state interests.[90] In particular, the twentieth-century emergence of Won Buddhism in Korea, with its synthesis of Buddhism, Ruism, and Daoism, and its overt focus on issues of social justice, is indicative of trends in Korean religious sensibilities during Iryŏp's lifetime.[91]

In this sense, then, Iryŏp's commitment to the social and political value of meditation aligns her existential thought with broadly Ruist concerns. And, in turn, Iryŏp's thought, as our starting point, has helped direct our own attention to the value of Ruist philosophy as existential philosophy. As mentioned throughout this book, there is a long history of comparative work focused on Buddhism, existentialism, and phenomenology, while the Ruist tradition has not received the same level of attention. That said, its influence in East Asian culture in general, and on Buddhism in particular, is often noted. For example, in Graham Parkes's various comparative works on Nietzsche, his focus is typically on Japanese Zen Buddhism and, to a lesser degree, Chinese Daoism, but he frequently contextualizes his discussion of Zen in light of pervasive East Asian philosophical assumptions about the nature and functioning of *qi*.[92]

Given that *qi*-philosophy in China is deeply rooted in the Ruist classic the *Yijing*, the work in this chapter builds on that heritage, seeking to highlight precisely the existential aspects of Ruist thought that come to the fore via its relation to *qi*-philosophy, not only the speculative work on *qi* and *li* that rises to prominence in the Song dynasty, but also a more traditional set of values dating back to the earlier texts as well. Through solicitude, seriousness, stillness, sincerity, and spontaneity, we find a vocabulary that addresses itself to the concrete practices of meaning-making.

"All must regard the cultivation of the self as the root."

From Kim Iryŏp's meditation as the emanation of "life-energy" to Zhu Xi's reading practices and *Yijing* divination, from the cultivation of seriousness and stillness to the manifestation of sincerity as a process of world-making, I hope I have shown that East Asian discourses in general, and Ruism in particular, offer us a compelling existential vision. In many ways, European existentialism in the twentieth century cannot be divorced from the specific dynamic of losing faith, by which

I mean both doubting the existence of the monotheistic creator of the Bible and losing confidence in the *telos* of progress associated with Enlightenment thought. East Asian intellectual history is not shaped by this particular trajectory of salvation, teleology, faith, and loss. Hence it does not frame the question of meaning, or articulate its fears over the absence of meaning, in ways that map onto European models.

In contrast to European nihilism, which concerns the breakdown of a particular realist sense of meaning or value, the Chinese tradition assumes the meaningfulness of existence but worries over the possible insignificance of human concerns in the larger cosmic context, over the inhospitableness of environmental or social orders that follow their own paths regardless of human attempts to intervene, and over the ultimate powerlessness of even the most highly cultivated moral exemplars. In response to these worries, we have seen an array of ritualistic and contemplative "existential coping strategies" that aim, at the most basic level, to help construct the sorts of selves who might, in turn, be able to reenter, revitalize, and recommit to the activity of meaningful world-creation. As the *Daxue* says, and as Zhu Xi emphatically believes, "All must regard the cultivation of the self as the root."[93] Hence, at the end of a book that has been critical toward or at least suspicious of the understanding of subjective interiority expressed in European existential philosophy, we nonetheless uphold the inner life of the mind as a source of transformative power. A speculative reconsideration of the existential meaning of "inner experience" is the subject of the concluding chapter.

Conclusion: Return to Inner Experience

Mystical states are available to me, if that is what I want. Maintaining my distance from beliefs, deprived of hopes, nothing compels me to enter these states .... Making my inner experience a project: doesn't that result in a remoteness, on my part, from the summit that might have been?

—Georges Bataille[1]

Over the course of this book, we have slowly redefined the contested category of "inner experience." A *qi*-based philosophy conceives of inner experience neither as the consciousness of a metaphysical subject nor as interiority in a strictly phenomenological sense. Rather, subjective life is explained in terms of either turbid or calm mental energies, which are not categorically different from bodily forms and physical matter in general. Turbid energies produce an agitated heart-mind, beset with tumultuous emotions, self-centered desires, and limited knowledge. Because of this agitated state, the heart-mind's activities are restricted to its own muddy and confused inner awareness. In contrast, specific techniques can calm the energies of the heart-mind, enabling an expansive awareness that extends beyond the borders of the body; as such, the calm heart-mind is capable of efficaciously intermixing with the energies of other people and the surrounding environment to meaningfully construct a shared world. The deepest sense of "inner experience," on a *qi*-based model, refers to the capacity of the heart-mind to relax into its primordial and undifferentiated state through meditative or contemplative practice.

Via the relinquishing of accumulated mental structures, the heart-mind can renew itself and replenish its fundamental creative potency.

Throughout the book, we have traced the impact of this *qi*-based understanding of mental phenomena on Buddhist, Ruist, and Daoist thought in East Asia, with reference to the specific practices that facilitate effects on both the microcosmic and macrocosmic scales. My goal has been to develop a "speculative existentialism" as a program for action—not a how-to guide for meaningful living but rather a philosophical methodology that takes seriously the power of self-cultivation, sustained by daily commitment, to enact existential transformation. And, in articulating this project, I have spoken as a reporter, not a practitioner. I will be the first to admit that I never find the time to meditate regularly, or even exercise; I am prone to feeling alienated; and I suffer from anxiety (not the liberating kind)—my heart-mind is undoubtedly agitated and my *qi* turbid. I can attest only that a wide range of philosophical traditions in East Asia assure me that another mode of awareness is possible, but I claim no firsthand experience.

Perhaps this is why I am continually drawn back to the quotation from Georges Bataille that opened this book in the introduction: "The sovereign desire of beings is what is beyond being. Anguish is the feeling of danger related to this inexhaustible expectation."[2] Although I see my own anxieties echoed in this passage, ultimately I think that Bataille's persistent orientation toward an ungraspable "beyond" is both exhausting and disempowering. And I remain convinced that a re-orientation of this "sovereign desire" requires us to see philosophical speculation and daily mind-body cultivation practices as two aspects of the same activity. What follows here, then, rather than a conclusion, is a "note to self"—a reminder, which I hope I will heed, that the transformative power of speculative philosophy exerts a mental energy that must be nourished, cultivated, and renewed daily.

The Partial Failure of Mysticism

After our extended focus on mostly Ruist views on *qi* and self-cultivation, I want to return to a comment by the Buddhist nun Kim Iryŏp, which opened the third chapter: "Anyone desirous of achieving [the great self] in this life should join a monastery, or, if that is not possible, one should practice concentration to attain the total power of mind. Only then will that person be free in her own actions."[3] Reflecting on Iryŏp's complete dedication to her life of monasticism, I found myself rereading Bataille's *Inner Experience*, a fretful and disjointed collection of writings on mystical and ascetic techniques, driven by his near-obsessive interest in transgressive experiences, both in theory and in practice. He was an avid researcher on topics of human sacrifice, sexual taboos, and torture, as well as asceticism, mysticism, and the sacred; and questions remain as to what extent he attempted to engage in such practices himself.[4] In *Inner Experience*, he takes up what he calls the method of "dramatization." It is unclear to me what he was actually doing, but he associates the technique with one of the "spiritual exercises" of St. Ignatius Loyola, which involves visualizing oneself undergoing the trial and execution of Jesus Christ.

Being Jewish, there is much that troubles me about this imaginative identification with Christ's agonies; accordingly, there is much that troubles me about Bataille in general. Pierre Klossowski is reported to have exclaimed upon hearing Bataille give a presentation, "You're just a Catholic."[5] In many ways, European philosophy as a whole cannot be divorced from the intellectual history of monotheism in the West, which, to be frank, perpetually causes me to doubt the viability of any comparative existential enterprise. Given these conflicted feelings, I was interested to find, upon rereading *Inner Experience*, a passage that jumped out to me for its affinity with the *qi*-based language I have been working with here. In it, Bataille describes his own consciousness as a multi-directional stream flowing inside as well as around him, establishing "warm" and "light" energetic connections to other beings:

> Further on, your life is not limited to that ungraspable inner streaming; it streams to the outside as well and opens itself incessantly to what flows out or surges forth towards it. The lasting vortex which constitutes you runs up against similar vortexes with which it forms a vast figure, animated by a measured agitation. Now to live signifies for you not only the flux and the fleeting play of light which are united in you, but the passage of warmth or of light from one being to another, from you to your fellow being or from your fellow being to you (even at the moment when you read in me the contagion of my fever which reaches you).[6]

In a work dominated by Bataille's feelings of isolation, alienation, and incommunicable turmoil, this passage stands out.

A few pages later, he continues this trajectory, recounting what he calls a "partly-failed" mystical experience. It begins with a shift in his consciousness as he sits on a veranda looking at the evening sky:

> Without giving these words more than an evocative value, I thought that the "sweetness of the sky" communicated itself to me and I could feel precisely the state within me which responded to it. I felt it to be present inside my head like a vaporous streaming, subtly graspable, but participating in the sweetness of the outside, putting me in possession of it, making me take pleasure in it.[7]

Here Bataille gives an uncharacteristically physicalist description of his consciousness as a "vaporous streaming" intermixing with the atmosphere around him. Together, these passages on multi-directional streaming and vaporous intermixing remind me of Zhu Xi's description, in a commentary on the *Daxue*, of the moment at which the heart-mind overflows the limited inner awareness of the petty person: "When you reach the point where you have exerted effort for a long time, there will be, all at once, sudden intermixing [*guantong* 貫通]. Then the outermost and innermost, the most refined and most coarse, in all the multitude of things will be attained."[8] In a telling comment on this passage, Joseph Adler describes *guantong* as the attainment of "existential freedom."[9]

So, why does Bataille consider his experience a partial failure? It seems it did not go far enough: "everything escapes if I have not been able to lose myself in Nothingness."[10] For Bataille, the ultimate transgression is not against this or that social norm, this or that moral dictate, this or that way of being, but against being itself—it is the inexhaustible desire for the "beyond of being"[11] that drives Bataille's experimentation with inner experience.

What does he mean by this "Nothingness" that is the "beyond of being"? He makes a fairly disturbing comment in *On Nietzsche*, where he explains the inevitable failure of all mystical experience as he conceives of it, which is as a "summit" moment followed by inevitable decline: "Just as in the last analysis the summit is simply inaccessible, from the start, decline is inevitable …. If the summit isn't death, the necessity of descent follows thereafter."[12] It is difficult to read this passage and not conclude that Bataille understands the idea of "losing himself in Nothingness" as simply dying. Judith Surkis comments that Bataille frequently places summit experiences related to eroticism, nothingness, and the "beyond of being" in a "zone of death"; although, as she also stresses, such experiences should in fact *not* be conflated with "absolute and final death": "The experience of death in eroticism is, by definition, always only proximate—simultaneously rupturing and maintaining the limits of individual existence."[13]

And this, for me, is precisely the problem—it is this suspension of the subject at an uncrossable border that I find both exhausting and disempowering. In conflating nothingness with the limit of a certain type of phenomenological interiority, death becomes a stand-in for all manner of trans-egoic experiences—losing oneself in another, losing oneself in God, losing oneself in the void or groundlessness of existence.

In an essay on Bataille, Foucault discusses the fascination with borders and limit experiences in recent philosophy, reflecting on Bataille's obsessive need to march himself right up to the edge in search of the ultimate transgression:

> Can the limit have a life of its own outside of the act that gloriously passes through it and negates it? For its part, does transgression not exhaust its nature when it crosses the limit, knowing no other life beyond this point in time? ... Transgression, then, is not related to the limit as black to white, the prohibited to the lawful, the outside to inside .... Rather, their relationship takes the form of a spiral which no simple infraction can exhaust.[14]

The limit experience becomes a "spiral" because no true crossing over is possible, when the subject aims (like Bataille) to "lose itself in Nothingness" only to find itself back in its old skin again and again. My own need to think through the ideas of nothingness and death from other perspectives is what put metaphysical speculation at the heart of this cross-cultural existential investigation.

The Impossibility of Nothingness

Although ideas of nothingness and emptiness have long been associated with East Asian thought, JeeLoo Liu unequivocally declares: "If we want to answer the question 'Why was there something rather than nothing?' we may reply that there is *something* exactly because there was never *nothing* .... in both classical Daoist and Neo-Confucian conceptions, there was no primordial absolute nothingness."[15]

Undoubtedly, by the Song dynasty, there were disagreements between Ruists, Daoists, and Buddhists over the question of "primordial absolute nothingness." In particular, Ruists accused Buddhists of fostering quietism, emotional detachment, and nihilism via their philosophical emphasis on emptiness, and often these critiques were extended to Daoist conceptions of nonbeing, as well. This was the stance we saw expressed in Hu Yuan's *Yijing* commentary in the third chapter. But Liu provides strong textual and etymological evidence to show that pre-Buddhist discourses in China find Ruists and Daoists closer together than they later appear. In a study of early Daoist texts, she points out that apparent references to nothingness or emptiness are in fact references to formlessness, which is to say, primordial formless *qi*. As a result, she asserts, both early Ruists and early Daoists share the same basic *qi*-cosmology in which utter nothingness is not a plausible metaphysical possibility. Accordingly, she argues that many Ruist critics of Daoism were often making a moral point about Daoist passivity; that is, they were mostly worried about the perceived abnegation of social responsibilities, not the ontological or cosmological status of nonbeing in anyone's metaphysical theory.

This perceived ethical danger in nothingness or emptiness continues growing stronger after the Song and Ming dynasties, as Ruist thought takes a philological turn, the philosophy of Zhu Xi and his generation comes to be viewed with suspicion, and a call is issued for a revival of the traditional moral philosophy of Mengzi (372–289 BCE). The Edo-period Japanese Ruist Kaibara Ekken (1630–1714) states in no uncertain terms: "To regard nothingness as the origin and fundamental spirit of all things is a Buddhist and Daoist idea. To regard existence as the origin and essence of all things is the teaching of the [Ruist] sages. Hence the explanations concerning existence and nonexistence are the dividing line between the Way of the sages and other paths."[16] He is particularly worried that Zhu Xi gives the impression that the cosmological origin or "Supreme Ultimate" (*taiji*

太極) is too similar to what the Buddhists mean by emptiness. In line with Liu's etymological point above, he criticizes the use of the single character (*zi* 子) for *wu* (無), implying "nothingness" itself, when it would be more correct to use *wu* in the compound meaning "formless" (*wuxing* 無形) instead: "If we wish to discuss the Supreme Ultimate, we should not first say the character for nothingness [*buke xian shuo wu zi* 不可先說無子]. The Supreme Ultimate is formless [*wuxing* 無形]; even a foolish person like myself understands that."[17] And, in line with Liu's overall argument, Ekken's main objection is a moral one. He worries that Buddhist influences on Ruism diminish what he sees as the properly Ruist understanding of *qi* as a life-giving source and the foundation for the uniquely human capacity of sincerity (*cheng* 誠).

Following Liu, I would say that Song-dynasty Ruist views on the question of formless *qi* have more in common with Ekken's own than he suggests; or, in other words, neither they nor the Daoists are as close to Buddhism as he accuses them of being.[18] And, in turn, Kim Iryŏp is certainly not the only Buddhist in East Asia whose understanding of emptiness was influenced by *qi*-based sensibilities. It is beyond the scope of this book to provide a historical study of the impact of South Asian Buddhist understandings of emptiness (*śūnyatā*) on indigenous Chinese traditions, and vice versa.[19] But, this project as a whole has been premised on the assertion that Kim Iryŏp's existential conception of emptiness as a type of formless "life-energy" is best understood within the framework of *qi*-cosmology, not Mahāyāna thought strictly speaking, which places her in a long line of East Asian thinkers, Buddhist and Ruist alike, who speak of emptiness as an inchoate, primal, creative source. Hence, from beginning to end, we have pursued an existential philosophy in which sheer emptiness is metaphysically implausible and nihilism is not a viable worldview.

As a result, Bataille's conflation of nothingness and the "beyond of being" would not make sense on a *qi*-based model, where there is no way to articulate anything beyond what Liu calls "an ever-present *qi*."[20] If we take Liu as our guide, then we cannot follow Bataille in saying that inner experience fails when it does not result in the total loss of the self to nothingness—on a *qi*-based model, there is no total loss to nothingness; there are only the polar tendencies of relaxing and dispersing, followed by gathering and solidifying, followed by relaxing again, and so on. There is no "summit" experience (to borrow Bataille's term) that is outside or beyond the continual back-and-forth of *qi*'s structural tendencies—formlessness is always already the beginning of new forms.

Bataille's views are admittedly extreme, but they are not unrelated to other general trajectories in European existentialism. The sharp border that he finds between being and the "beyond of being" reflects the tenor of phenomenology as a whole, which is premised on a capacity to identify the limits beyond which experience cannot venture. Heidegger's account of death as the "possibility of the impossibility of any existence at all"[21] is precisely such an outer limit—the eventual nonexistence of the experiencing subject is a moment that, by definition, is impossible to experience. As for the question of personal death, I obviously propose no answers. But I cannot help but think that such phenomenological limit experiences lose some of their force in a *qi*-based philosophy, where inner life knows no sharp border beyond which fluid intermixing cannot occur. Surely, it is this capacity for ever-vital transformation and renewal that led so many Ruists to see themselves as offering a life-affirming counterpoint to Buddhism's philosophy of emptiness.

Sagehood and the Limits of Subjectivity

One can argue (rightly, I think) that the Ruist critiques of Buddhism are at times unfair; or, in other words, Buddhist emptiness is not the simplistic nihilism that Ruist critics often make it out to be. On the one hand, some Buddhist accounts of enlightenment experiences do seem to have more to contribute to a conversation with Bataille on what it means to lose the self to nothingness. For example, Ekken's younger contemporary, the Buddhist monk Hakuin (1686–1768), speaks of nirvāṇa as the "great death"—perhaps it is language such as this that troubled Ruists like Ekken. On the other hand, upon closer inspection, the Edo-period Zen master certainly did not conceive of the "great death" as a total loss to nothingness or a summit followed by inevitable decline. As Gereon Kopf says succinctly, "The practitioner does not attain 'enlightenment' (*satori* 悟り) in the once-in-a-lifetime experience Zen Master Hakuin 白隠慧鶴 (1686–1768) likens to the 'great death' (*daishi* 大死) but 'actualizes' (*shōsuru* 證する) buddhahood every moment anew in daily practice."[22] Even in Hakuin's "great death," then, we see echoes of Iryŏp's own account of emptiness as a source of creativity and renewal.

Given the complex philosophical studies of emptiness that we find in the Chan lineages of East Asia, it is no surprise that European philosophers have been interested in Buddhism or that recent East Asian philosophers, such as the Kyoto School, have been interested in European phenomenology and existentialism. And just as I think the Ruist critics can be said to be overly harsh in their assessment of Buddhism, I do not suggest here that European existentialism is naively nihilistic (and I hope the bulk of the work in this book attests to that). But, the Ruist approach to the question of emptiness, rooted in a *qi*-based philosophy, brings new perspectives to cross-cultural existential work. The Ruist figure of the sage in particular underscores the departure we have taken from Bataille, and perhaps, the departure we have taken from the conventions of phenomenological bracketing. In other words, to take the idea of sagehood seriously as an existential possibility, we necessarily speculate regarding realities that exceed the experiential capacities of the subject as ordinarily understood.

In early Ruist sources, at least three model personalities are mentioned, including "scholar-apprentices" (*shi* 士), exemplary persons (*junzi* 君子), and sages (*shengren* 聖人); these, by the time of Xunzi (*c*. third century BCE), are linked together hierarchically as stages of self-cultivation.[23] By the Song dynasty, scholars spoke in more pedagogical language of "lesser learning" (*xiaoxue* 小學) for children and young teens followed by "greater learning" (*daxue* 大學) for older teens and adults. The former included training in "ritual, music, archery, charioteering, calligraphy, and mathematics,"[24] while the latter included the practices of reading, contemplation, and cultivated seriousness associated with the *Daxue*'s program of self-development. In between the two stages, as Stephen C. Angle describes, comes a period of establishing commitment, or the setting of one's intention to strive for sagehood.[25]

This is only the beginning, as Angle says, of a long path of ever-deepening and maturing commitment:

> At many points the Confucian program generates empirical feedback that further deepens one's commitment to it: one *can* increasingly come to see possibilities for harmony, and these possibilities can, at least sometimes, be realized. There are even moments in which one can see flashes of interconnections that constitute universal coherence [*li* 理]: these are "enlightenment (*wu* 悟)" experiences that many Neo-Confucians report …. such experiences do not (at least for the strand of Neo-Confucianism I am endorsing) constitute the arrival of sagehood, nor the end of the process of development, but they do help push one further along the path.[26]

On this model, there is no summit and decline, no sharp border between the present and the great beyond, but rather an ever-deepening progressive development of one's capacities for existential engagement and realization. There is both "empirical feedback," as Angle says, which confirms the expansion of mental powers and attests to what the subject is capable of experiencing; but there are also "flashes" of something more—not the "beyond of being" but certainly beyond what the subject in its present form is able to fully grasp. Being open to speculation, in this sense, means the humbleness to acknowledge modes of awareness beyond one's current abilities.

All of this, from beginning to end, is made possible by practice. As the Ruist tradition consistently makes clear, there is simply no substitute for diligent daily practice, including contemplative quiet-sitting, the method of seriousness, and the transformative pursuit of reading and scholarship. Subjectivity remains petty or small (*xiao* 小) without these practices that enable its expansion, and only practices can provide the confirmation via "empirical feedback" that other modes of awareness are indeed possible. This is why, as I say above, philosophical speculation and daily mind-body cultivation practices are two aspects of the same activity. And of all the practices we have covered, philosophical reading remains the closest to my own commitments and experiences.

The Communion of Inner Life

> *Here's what is necessary: one blow with a club, one scar; one slap on the face, a handful of blood. Experience other people's writings just like this. You must not turn away!*
>
> —Zhu Xi[27]

Evoking the possibility of philosophical communion via text, in *Inner Experience* Bataille contemplates: "Thus we are nothing, neither you nor I, beside burning words which could pass from me to you, imprinted on a page."[28] In an interesting, if unintentional, counterpoint to Bataille's work, the great twentieth-century Chinese philosopher Tu Weiming titles a 1976 article "'Inner Experience': The Basis of Creativity in Neo-Confucian Thinking."[29] There, he selects the term "inner experience" to refer to a cluster of Chinese compounds using the character *ti* (體), all of which refer to various species of embodied awareness. He draws a distinction between inner experience and what he calls "a solipsistic state," pointing out that attaining inner experience, in the Chinese sense of the term, means overcoming ordinary subjective consciousness.[30] Notably, he holds that inner experience is simultaneously a "spiritual communion" (*shenhui* 神會) with others, both living and dead, especially in that reading classical texts allows us to commune with the sages of the past. But, he clarifies, communion with the spirit of a text does not imply simply fidelity to authority:

> Transmission in a real sense always implies an act of creativity—not creating something out of nothing, to be sure, but deepening one's self-awareness to the extent that its quality is comparable to that of the ancients .... When 'inner experience' is conceived as the basis of creativity, the art of constructing some philosophical system *ex nihilo*, no matter how ingenious (*ch'iao*) it may be, cannot be accepted as profound.[31]

Tu's resistance to the idea of philosophical creation ex nihilo takes us back to Liu's work on the question of nothingness versus formlessness in East Asian thought. Like the *Yijing* commentators we saw in the third chapter, whose metaphysical objections to nothingness shaped their understanding of how new values are created, Tu's understanding of meaning and creativity seems to be informed by the underlying sensibility that something cannot, and never has, come from nothing.

In place of any romantic notion of philosophical originality, Tu invokes the power of interpersonal and transgenerational "spiritual communion." Like Zhu Xi, Tu upholds philosophical reading as a special, intimate, transformative experience. Its profundity lies in depths that exceed a single thinker, no matter how original, and its trajectory reaches new heights unattainable on the basis of tradition alone, no matter how much the past is revered. Tu's comments resonate with many of the main themes in this book as a whole—i.e., the idea that "inner experience" is simultaneously communion, personal creativity is simultaneously the product of tradition, and the self's existential freedom is simultaneously the spontaneous expression of ongoing structural tendencies in the matter–energy matrix of existence itself.

At the end of his essay "Spiritual Exercises," Hadot says that he will be satisfied if his work encourages people to appreciate a few "old truths" and the necessity of reading for themselves the old books that contain them.[32] I certainly cannot imagine ending a book on the question of meaning in life by saying anything new. All that I have discussed here only underscores the time-honored truth that reading and learning, education and scholarship, are vital to human meaning-making and value-creation. What inspires me the most in this cross-cultural turn, however, is the promise of "spiritual communion" that Tu invokes. The meeting of minds, the exchange of energies (or drives, Nietzsche might say), the transformative interactions of *qi*-based subjectivities—all such possibilities are contained in the vision for existential realization that East Asian traditions express. Reading is transformative, to be sure, and East Asian philosophies ask us to treat these inner transformations with *seriousness*. They ask us to take seriously the possibility that our private thoughts and feelings are not so safely contained; that our inner lives manifest outwardly, as well; and that these outward-bound forces may easily defy our control so long as we lack training. But, with practice and commitment, we can indeed progress toward the expanded subjectivity signaled by the figure of the sage. My hope upon conclusion is that this book might speak to others who, like me, are at times exhausted in the face of persistent existential uncertainties, and who find in the promise of philosophical communion a source of creative renewal.

Notes

Introduction

1 Bataille, *On Nietzsche*, 22.
2 See Hadot, *Philosophy as a Way of Life: Spiritual Exercises from Socrates to Foucault*.
3 Ibid., 108.
4 This is not quite accurate, and I will better contextualize this claim as the book progresses. Bataille himself experimented with a range of mystical practices, and Michel Foucault, being inspired by Hadot's work, looked to Greek, Roman, and Christian practices as technologies for subjective development. But, as we will see, many such practices give us a picture of the self that is indebted to the very metaphysics of (spiritual) subject and (material) object that existential philosophy seeks to overcome. Overall, if we are looking for a systematic account of daily practices, both personal and social, that relate to enacting the vision of trans-egoic meaning-making expressed in existential theory, we will not find it within existential writings themselves.
5 This is borrowed from the terminology used in discussions of Chinese medicine as well as aesthetic practices such as gardening or architecture. See, for example, Graham Parkes, "Winds, Waters, and Earth Energies: *Fengshui* and Awareness of Place," in the collection *Nature across Cultures: Views of Nature and the Environment in Non-Western Cultures*, or James Miller, "Daoism and Nature," in the same collection.
6 One obvious question is whether this account of mental life is scientifically plausible. The central underlying concept that grounds this account of the mind, as will be introduced soon, is the Chinese notion of *qi* (氣), the matter-energy matrix that characterizes all existing things as well as existence itself. Some philosophers do attempt to connect *qi*-based philosophy with contemporary science. See, for example,

JeeLoo Liu's article "Chinese *Qi*-Naturalism and Liberal Naturalism." I am deeply interested in this sort of work, although I make no attempt here to justify a *qi*-based picture of the mind with reference to scientific literature. As Owen Flanagan comments, in *The Really Hard Problem: Meaning in a Material World*: "No one … has yet explained consciousness. What we have are pictures of how we might explain it, and differing assessments about how far along various research programs are in the attempt to explain how and why experiences occur" (26). Flanagan is convinced that philosophical naturalism is best aligned with scientific evidence. Although I am not so strongly committed to naturalism, I hold open the possibility that a *qi*-based model may indeed accord with a naturalistic worldview. This is certainly Nicholas Brasovan's position in his book *Neo-Confucian Ecological Humanism*, which heavily informs my work in the third chapter.

7   One of the key texts in the field, Quentin Meillassoux's *After Infinitude*, is discussed in the second chapter.

8   For example, Whitehead, *Process and Reality*.

9   See Shaviro, *Without Criteria: Kant, Whitehead, Deleuze, and Aesthetics*. In this book, Shaviro imagines what contemporary postmodern thought might look like if Whitehead, not Heidegger, had been the more influential figure.

10 For an extended discussion, see the editors' Introduction to *Chinese Metaphysics and Its Problems* by Chenyang Li and Franklin Perkins.

11 Throughout the book, I make use of the digital database Chinese Text Project at ctext.org. Developed by Donald Sturgeon, this open-access library is the largest online repository of classical and literary Chinese-language texts and is cross-referenced with multiple established concordances (https://ctext.org/tools/concordance). As of 2016, it contains over 5 million scanned pages from the Harvard Yenching Library, including images from its Chinese Rare Books Collection. That said, the Chinese Text Project would not be the first choice for sinologists or others engaged in advanced philological or linguistic work, who would choose to cite a concordance directly. For my purposes here, the Chinese Text Project well suffices.

12 Baba, "*Zhijue* as Appreciation and Realization in Zhu Xi: An Examination through Hun and Po," 302.
13 See especially chapters 1 and 2 of Jason Ānanda Josephson, *The Invention of Religion in Japan*.
14 *Lunyu* 論語, 3.14, https://ctext.org/analects/zh. In this passage, Kongzi famously declares himself a follower of the ways of the Zhou dynasty (1046–256 BCE).
15 Godart, "'Philosophy' or 'Religion'? The Confrontation with Foreign Categories in Late Nineteenth Century Japan," 76.
16 I use "buddha" in lowercase to refer to the generic category of enlightened beings, but retain capital letters when using the term as an honorific title after a name, such as Śākyamuni Buddha.
17 For more context on my use of these terms as categories for contemporary cross-cultural scholarship, see Kalmanson, "Dharma and Dao: Key Terms in the Comparative Philosophy of Religion."
18 I follow traditional convention of referring to Kim by her dharma name Iryŏp.
19 Similarly, Greek and Roman "spiritual practices" cannot be neatly divorced from metaphysical theories that underlie them. On this issue, see Aaron Stalnaker's engagement with the work of Hadot in *Overcoming Our Evil: Human Nature and Spiritual Exercises in Xunzi and Augustine*, 33–4. See also Stephen Angle's comments on Stalnaker's work and his discussion of the question of reviving ancient practices in contemporary times in *Sagehood*, 145.
20 For example, Keiji Nishitani, *The Self-Overcoming of Nihilism*; Graham Parkes, editor of *Nietzsche and Asian Thought* and *Heidegger and Asian Thought*; Bret Davis, "Zen after Zarathustra: The Problem of the Will in the Confrontation between Nietzsche and Buddhism"; and Jason Wirth, *Nietzsche and Other Buddhas*.
21 Given that much of the second chapter is devoted to the topic of Buddhism and meaning-making, one book that deserves discussion, introduced above at note 6, is *The Really Hard Problem: Meaning in a Material World* by Owen Flanagan. In it, he draws connections between Buddhist philosophy, neuroscience, moral psychology, mindfulness

studies, and evolutionary biology to give a purely naturalistic account of human meaning-making. As I say above, I myself am not so committed to naturalism, or, at least, I am not so convinced that I know where to draw the line between the natural and the so-called supernatural. As will become clear in the second chapter, I engage precisely those seemingly supernatural aspects of Buddhist philosophy that Flanagan, for the most part, avoids.

22 For example, Stephen Angle and Justin Tiwald, *Neo-Confucianism: A Philosophical Introduction*.
23 For example, Daniel Gardner, trans., *Learning to Be a Sage*.
24 For example, P. J. Ivanhoe, *Three Streams: Confucian Reflections on Learning and the Moral Heart-Mind in China, Korea, and Japan*.
25 In earliest uses, *li* means to cut and polish jade—this is the inspiration for the image chosen for the cover of the book, *Green Key* (2019) by Christopher Chiavetta (courtesy of Olson-Larsen Galleries). A carver of jade must follow the structure characteristic of a specific piece of stone, to split it along the right lines, and then polish it to further reveal the pattern of striations. See Brook Ziporyn, *Beyond Oneness and Difference*, 28–9, for a discussion of earliest definitions of *li*, and 330 for a discussion of Zhu Xi's reference to *li* and its early meanings.
26 Zhu Xi 朱熹, *Zhuzi yulei* 朱子語類, "Li qi shang" 理氣上, http://ctext.org/zhuzi-yulei/1/zh#n586150 (天下未有無理之氣，亦未有無氣之理). See Gardner's translation in *Learning to Be a Sage*, 90.
27 *Daxue* 大學, https://ctext.org/liji/da-xue/zh (古之欲明明德於天下者，先治其國；欲治其國者，先齊其家；欲齊其家者，先修其身；欲修其身者，先正其心；欲正其心者，先誠其意；欲誠其意者，先致其知，致知在格物。物格而後知至，知至而後意誠，意誠而後心正，心正而後身修，身修而後家齊，家齊而後國治，國治而後天下平。自天子以至於庶人，壹是皆以修身為本). See Ian Johnston's and Wang Ping's translation in *Daxue and Zhongyong*, 45–7 and 135.
28 Rošker, *Traditional Chinese Thought and the Paradigm of Structure (Li* 理*)*, 103.
29 See Joseph Adler, "Varieties of Spiritual Experience: *Shen* in Neo-Confucian Discourse."

30 Lazzarato, *Signs and Machines*, 44.
31 See, for example, *Beyond Good and Evil*, especially the first chapter "On the Prejudices of Philosophers," and *On the Genealogy of Morality*, III, 12.
32 See, for example, Catriona Mackenzie and Natalie Stoljar, eds., *Relational Autonomy: Feminist Perspectives on Autonomy, Agency, and the Social Self*.
33 Foucault, "Technologies of the Self," 19.
34 Ibid., 37.
35 Much of the contemporary work on Nietzsche remains stuck (as we see in the next chapter) on hashing out the differences between subjective preferences and objective values. See, for example, Neil Sinhababu and Brian Leiter, eds., *Nietzsche and Morality*, for several chapters debating the finer points of Nietzsche's views on values, objectivity, and creativity. More recently, see also Harold Langsam, "Nietzsche and Value Creation: Subjectivism, Self-Expression, and Strength"; Maudemarie Clark, "Nietzsche and Value Creation"; and Manuel Dries, "How Hard Is It to Create Values?"
36 For example, works by Nishitani, Parkes, Davis, and Wirth in note 20 above.
37 Parkes, "Open Letter to Bret Davis—Letter on Egoism: Will to Power as Interpretation," 59. Parkes's note (page 69, note 38) on the references in the cited passage is as follows: "Z IV: 'The Drunken Song,' IV: 'At Midday,' III: 'On Old and New Tablets' 19; *Mencius* 2A2, trans. D. C. Lau (London: Penguin, 2004), 32–3; *Zhuangzi*, chap. 4; Nishitani, *The Self-Overcoming of Nihilism*, trans. Graham Parkes and Setsuko Aihara (Albany: State University of New York Press, 1990), 50."
38 Nietzsche, *The Gay Science*, 346.

Chapter 1

1 Kant, *Critique of Pure Reason*, Preface to the Second Edition, B XL (page 121 in the Guyer and Wood translation).
2 Heidegger, *Being and Time*, translated by John Macquarrie and Edward Robinson, 249.

3   In the recently published *Galileo's Error* (2019), Philip Goff attributes the roots of this scandal to the "father of modern science" Galileo (1564–1642), who sought to restrict science to mathematically quantifiable phenomena. As Goff argues, "Galileo's error was to commit us to a theory of nature which entailed that consciousness was essentially and inevitably mysterious. In other words, Galileo created the problem of consciousness" (21–2). Goff's solution to this error is a sustained defense of panpsychism. Although I am unable to fully engage his argument here, his speculative claim (via a discussion of mysticism) that "formless consciousness is the ultimate nature of *physical reality*" (207) does suggest interesting overlap with the notion of primordial undifferentiated *qi* (*yuanqi* 元氣) introduced in the third chapter.

4   See, for example, Wolf, "Happiness and Meaning: Two Aspects of the Good Life," *Meaning in Life and Why It Matters*, and "Meaningfulness: A Third Dimension in the Good Life." I am quoting from an excerpt of Wolf's "Happiness and Meaning" article appearing in the chapter "Meaning in Life" in *The Meaning of Life: A Reader*, edited by E. D. Klemke and Steven M. Cahn, 232.

5   Wolf, "Meaning in Life," 232.

6   Ibid., 233.

7   Cahn, "Meaningless Lives?" 237.

8   Qtd. in ibid., 237.

9   Ibid., 233.

10 Aquinas, *Questiones Disputatae de Veritate*, Question 1, Article III.

11 Blackburn, *The Oxford Dictionary of Philosophy*, 244.

12 Ibid.

13 See, for example, *Beyond Good and Evil*, especially the first chapter "On the Prejudices of Philosophers," and *On the Genealogy of Morality*, III, 12.

14 Gregg, "Reflections on the Feminist Critique of Objectivity," 9.

15 Wilson, *The Meaning of Human Existence*, 15.

16 Ibid., 13–14.

17 Ibid., 174.

18 Ibid., 173.
19 Ibid., 173.
20 Ibid., 173–4.
21 Ibid., 181.
22 Ibid., 180–1.
23 Descartes, *Meditations on First Philosophy*, 17–18.
24 Ibid., 29.
25 See, for example, Hobbes, *Elements of Law*, Part I, chapter 1, and Locke, *An Essay Concerning Human Understanding*.
26 See Berkeley, *Treatise Concerning the Principles of Human Knowledge*.
27 Hume, *An Enquiry Concerning Human Understanding*, especially sections 4 and 5.
28 Hume, *Treatise of Human Nature*, 1.4.6.3.
29 Kant, *Critique of Pure Reason*, B xvi.
30 For a full account of his argument, see the *Critique of Pure Reason*, especially the Transcendental Aesthetic and Transcendental Analytic.
31 Ibid., A 51/B 74.
32 Ibid., A 346/B 404.
33 Nietzsche, *Thus Spoke Zarathustra*, 30.
34 Ibid., 52.
35 Ibid., 52.
36 Parkes, "Open Letter to Bret Davis—Letter on Egoism: Will to Power as Interpretation," 45.
37 Langsam, "Nietzsche and Value Creation: Subjectivism, Self-Expression, and Strength," 101.
38 Hussain, "Honest Illusion: Valuing for Nietzsche's Free Spirits," 157.
39 Ibid., 178.
40 Huddleston, "Nietzsche's Meta-Axiology: Against the Sceptical Readings," 323.
41 Silk, "Nietzschean Constructivism: Ethics and Metaethics for All and None," 253.
42 Clark and Dudrick, "Nietzsche and Moral Objectivity: The Development of Nietzsche's Metaethics," 225.
43 Poellner, "Affect, Value, and Objectivity," 227.

44 Heidegger, *Being and Time*. The phrase is introduced in Division One, Part One, Chapter One "The Exposition of the Task of a Preparatory Analysis of *Dasein*" and a full explication of the idea occupies all of Chapters Two to Six.
45 Beauvoir, *Ethics of Ambiguity*, 159.
46 Ibid., 28
47 Ibid., 129
48 Ibid., 159.
49 Ibid., 156.
50 Ibid., 156.
51 Ibid., 157.
52 Meillassoux, *After Finitude*, 50.
53 Ibid.
54 Sparrow, *The End of Phenomenology*, 189.
55 Ibid., 70.
56 Ibid., 69.
57 Ibid.
58 Ibid., 188.
59 Ibid., 189.

Chapter 2

1 Bataille, *On Nietzsche*, xxvii.
2 Kim Iryŏp, *Reflections of a Zen Buddhist Nun*, 41.
3 See the discussion of the hammer in Heidegger, *Being and Time*, Part One, Division One, Chapter Three, section 15 "The Being of Beings Encountered in the Surrounding World" (Joan Stambaugh translation).
4 Bataille, *The Accursed Share*, 23.
5 Ibid.
6 Ibid.
7 Ibid., 24.
8 Ibid., 108–9.
9 Ibid.

10 As he says, "For a generation delighting in worldly attachment, that takes delight in worldly attachment, and rejoices in worldly attachment, this doctrine is hard to see, namely, dependent arising which involves specific conditionality." He at first concludes that he will keep his realization private, but a manifestation of the god Brahmā convinces him to share the dharma with others. See Holder, *Early Buddhist Discourses*, 9.

11 Ibid., 65–6.

12 Ibid., 29. See also the Nagara Sutta, where the Buddha explains: "Then the thought occurred to me, 'Consciousness exists when what exists? From what as a requisite condition comes consciousness?' From my appropriate attention there came the breakthrough of discernment: 'Consciousness exists when name-&-form [psycho-physicality] exists. From name-&-form as a requisite condition comes consciousness.' Then the thought occurred to me, 'This consciousness turns back at name-&-form, and goes no farther. It is to this extent that there is birth, aging, death, falling away, & re-arising, i.e., from name-&-form as a requisite condition comes consciousness, from consciousness as a requisite condition comes name-&-form. From name-&-form as a requisite condition come the six sense media …. Thus is the origination of this entire mass of stress. Origination, origination.' Vision arose, clear knowing arose, discernment arose, knowledge arose, illumination arose within me with regard to things never heard before"; Thanissaro Bhikkhu, "Nagara Sutta: The City," https://www.accesstoinsight.org/tipitaka/sn/sn12/sn12.065.than.html.

13 Thanissaro Bhikkhu, "The Truth of Rebirth and Why It Matters for Buddhist Practice," part 4, https://www.accesstoinsight.org/lib/authors/thanissaro/truth_of_rebirth.html.

14 Holder, *Early Buddhist Discourses*, 9.

15 Ibid., 119.

16 See, for example, the sutra on the foundations of mindfulness (*Mahāsatipaṭṭhāna Sutta*) in the fourth chapter of Holder, *Early Buddhist Discourses*.

17 I borrow this description from Eric S. Nelson's book review "Kim Iryŏp's Existential Buddhism: Book Review of Jin Y. Park, trans. and

introduction, *Reflections of a Zen Buddhist Nun: Essays by Zen Master Kim Iryŏp*."

18 Jiemin Bao, "Merit-Making: Capitalism Re-territorializing Thai Buddhism in Silicon Valley, California."
19 Ibid., 128.
20 For a detailed account of the rise and fall of the Sanjie movement, see chapters seven and eight of Hubbard, *Absolute Delusion*.
21 Wendi Adamek, *Mystique of Transmission*, 127.
22 Ibid., 211. Even during its years of successful operation, it faced suppressions by several emperors (and Empress Wu). See Hubbard, *Absolute Delusion*, 190.
23 See Teresina Rowell, *The Background and Early Use of the Buddha-Kṣetra Concept*, Introduction and Chapter One.
24 Shinran, *The Collected Works of Shinran, Volume 1*, 663.
25 Ibid., 260.
26 Curley, Melissa Anne-Marie, *Pure Land/Real World*, 23.
27 Foulk, "Ritual in Japanese Zen Buddhism," 64.
28 Bhikkhu Bodhi, ed., *In the Buddha's Words*, 100.
29 The language of "first cause" is my own. As the text puts it, we cannot count back in time "This is my mother, this is my mother's mother," for "the sequence ... of mothers and grandmothers would not come to an end." See Bhikkhu Bodhi, *In the Buddha's Words*, 100.
30 Kim Iryŏp, *Reflections of a Zen Buddhist Nun: Essays by Zen Master Kim Iryŏp*, 221.
31 Ibid.
32 See Jin Y. Park, *Women and Buddhist Philosophy: Engaging Zen Master Kim Iryŏp*, "Introduction," for a full discussion of Iryŏp's life.
33 Ibid., 38.
34 Ibid., 34.
35 Ibid.
36 Iryŏp joined the nunnery at Sudeoksa temple, head temple of the Jogye order of Korean Seon Buddhism.
37 I consulted the Chinese version of Huineng's second chapter "Prajñā" (*bore* 般若) of the *Platform Sutra of the Sixth Patriarch* (*liuzutanjing* 六祖壇經) at https://ctext.org/wiki.pl?if=gb&chapter=459983.

38 Cleary, trans., *The Sutra of Hui-neng*, 16, with my modifications (若見一切法，心不染著，是為無念。用即徧一切處，亦不著一切處 […] 來去自由，通用無滯 […] 名無念行).
39 Ibid. (若百物不思，當令念絕，即是法縛，即名邊見).
40 Ibid., 17 (第一莫著空，若空心靜坐，即著無記空).
41 Ibid. (善知識，世界虛空，能含萬物色像。日月星宿，山河大地、泉源溪澗、草木叢林、惡人善人、惡法善法、天堂地獄、一切大海、須彌諸山、總在空中；世人性空，亦復如是。善知識，自性能含萬法是大，萬法在諸人性中).
42 Kim Iryŏp, *Reflections of a Zen Buddhist Nun*, 30.
43 Park, "Translator's Introduction: Kim Iryŏp, Her Life and Thought," 1. For more on Iryŏp's fraught relationship with her writing practice, see Park, *Women and Buddhist Philosophy: Engaging Zen Master Kim Iryŏp*, especially pages 175 to 179 of the section titled "Writing, Buddhist Practice, and the Production of Meaning."
44 Kim Iryŏp, *Reflections of a Zen Buddhist Nun*, 93.
45 Ibid., 90.
46 Ibid., 38.
47 Ibid., 54.
48 Ibid., 219.
49 Ibid., 38.
50 Ibid., 52.
51 Ibid., 49 and 53.
52 Ibid., 51.
53 Ibid., 217. *Saengmyŏng* is the Korean pronunciation of the Chinese *shengming* (生命) referring the lifespan, or allotted span of vitality, accorded a single living organism. Kim, in using this word, not only expands the Buddhist framework but also accomplishes a feminist appropriation of *saengmyŏng*, which, as Jae-Yon Lee discusses, was a popular literary and aesthetic term in the 1920s. In particular, it was used to describe the creative genius of the artist, who invigorates his artworks through the power of his own vitality. Lee describes the views of literary author Kim Tongin on women and creativity: "Kim Tongin contested that, historically, such creative minds were only granted to men who built up the world of convenience by exploiting inconvenient

nature. A woman, on the other hand, had the power of imitation and the courage to blindly pursue her goals. Kim lamented that such power also misguided women into believing in the ideology of gender equality and claiming their right to vote. He acerbically criticized this claim because, he argued, women possess neither spirit nor creative power." Lee, "Authors as Creators of Art: The Collaborative Shaping of Literary Writers in *Ch'angjo*," 89.

54 Kim Iryŏp, *Reflections of a Zen Buddhist Nun*, 218.
55 Ibid., 220.
56 Ibid., 89.
57 Ibid., 234.
58 I follow Stephen C. Angle in translating *tian* as "cosmos." See Angle, "*Tian* as Cosmos in Zhu Xi's Neo-Confucianism." For more on the influence of pre-Buddhist Chinese *qi*-based views on Buddhist thought, see Robert Sharf, *Coming to Terms with Chinese Buddhism: A Reading of the* Treasure Store Treatise, especially the second chapter, "Chinese Buddhism and the Cosmology of Sympathetic Resonance."
59 Kim Iryŏp, *Reflections of a Zen Buddhist Nun*, 220.
60 Ibid., 221.

Chapter 3

1 *Yijing* 易經, *Xici xia* 繫辭下, https://ctext.org/book-of-changes/xi-ci-xia/zh (古者包犧氏之王天下也，仰則觀象於天，俯則觀法於地，觀鳥獸之文，與地之宜，近取諸身，遠取諸物，於是始作八卦，以通神明之德，以類萬物之情).
2 Kundera, *Immortality*, 227.
3 Kundera, *The Unbearable Lightness of Being*, 14.
4 Ibid.
5 Qtd. in Baba, "*Zhijue* as Appreciation and Realization in Zhu Xi: An Examination through Hun and Po," 310 (parenthetical Chinese terms in Baba's original). See the Chinese version at Zhu Xi 朱熹, *Zhuzi yulei* 朱子語類, 禮四 (*lisi*), 小戴禮 (*xiaodaili*), 祭義 (*jiyi*), passage 5, https://ctext.org/text.pl?node=597170&if=en (陰主藏受，陽主運用。凡能記憶，

皆魄之所藏受也，至於運用發出來是魂。這兩箇物事本不相離。他能記憶底是魄，然發出來底便是魂；能知覺底是魄，然知覺發出來底又是魂。雖各自分屬陰陽，然陰陽中又各自有陰陽也).

6. Baba, "*Zhijue* as Appreciation and Realization in Zhu Xi: An Examination through *Hun* and *Po*," 311.
7. James Miller, *China's Green Religion: Daoism and the Quest for a Sustainable Future*, 35.
8. Parkes, *Composing the Soul*, 286–88.
9. Kim, "Zhu Xi on Scientific and Occult Subjects: Defining and Extending the Boundaries of Confucian Learning," 129.
10. Adler, "Varieties of Spiritual Experience: *Shen* in Neo-Confucian Discourse," 141.
11. Ibid., 134.
12. Zhu Xi 朱熹, *Zhuzi yulei* 朱子語類, 學四, (*xuesi*), 讀書法上 (*dushufashang*), passage 65, https://ctext.org/zhuzi-yulei/10/zh (書只貴讀，讀多自然曉). In general, my translations follow Gardner, trans., *Learning to Be a Sage*; see 137.
13. Zhu Xi, *Zhuzi yulei*, 學四 (*xuesi*), 讀書法上 (*dushufashang*), passage 65, https://ctext.org/zhuzi-yulei/10/zh (這箇不知如何，自然心與氣合，舒暢發越，自是記得牢); see Gardner, trans., 137–8.
14. Zhu Xi, *Zhuzi yulei*, 學五 (*xuewu*), 讀書法下 (*dushufaxia*), passage 21, https://ctext.org/zhuzi-yulei/11/zh (學者讀書，須要斂身正坐，緩視微吟，虛心涵泳); see Gardner, trans., 147.
15. Zhu Xi, *Zhuzi yulei*, 學五 (*xuewu*), 讀書法下 (*dushufaxia*), passage 12, https://ctext.org/zhuzi-yulei/11/zh (今且要讀書，須先定其心，使之如止水，如明鏡); see Garder, trans., 145.
16. Zhu Xi, *Zhuzi yulei*, 學五 (*xuewu*), 讀書法下 (*dushufaxia*), passage 12, https://ctext.org/zhuzi-yulei/11/zh (心不定，故見理不得); see Garder, trans., 145.
17. *Guanzi* 管子, *Neiye* 內業, passage 2, http://ctext.org/guanzi/nei-ye (心靜氣理，道乃可止). For my translations I consulted Rickett's translation in *Guanzi: Political, Economic, and Philosophical Essays from Early China*, vol. 2; see page 41.
18. *Guanzi*, *Neiye*, passage 1, http://ctext.org/guanzi/nei-ye (是故此氣也，不可止以力， 而可安以德); see Rickett, trans., vol. 2, 39.

19. *Guanzi, Jie* 戒, https://ctext.org/guanzi/jie (所以謂德者。不動而疾，不相告而知，不為而成，不召而至，是德也。故天不動，四時云下，而萬物化；君不動，政令陳下，而萬功成；心不動，使四肢耳目，而萬物情); see Rickett, trans., vol. 1, 379.
20. See JeeLoo Liu, *Neo-Confucianism: Metaphysics, Mind, and Morality*, especially Part I.
21. Anecdotally, I would note that that standard Japanese greeting "*Ogenki desu ka*" (お元気ですか) is an inquiry about the current state of your primordial *qi*. (The Japanese character *ki* 気 is a simplified form of the older Chinese *qi* 氣).
22. *Guanzi, Neiye*, passage 3, http://ctext.org/guanzi/nei-ye (凡心之形，過知失生); Rickett, trans., vol. 2, 44.
23. *Guanzi, Xinshu xia* 心術下, passage 3, https://ctext.org/guanzi/xin-shu-ii (極變者，所以應物也。慕選而不亂，極變而不煩，執一之君子。執一而不失，能君萬物。日月之與同光，天地之與同理); see Rickett, trans., vol. 2, 60–1.
24. *Guanzi, Neiye*, passage 5, http://ctext.org/guanzi/nei-ye (心以藏心，心之中又有心焉。彼心之心，音/意 以先言，音/意 然後形，形然後言。言然後使，使然後治。不治必亂，亂乃死); see Rickett, trans., vol. 2, 46–7.
25. *Guanzi, Neiye*, passage 1, http://ctext.org/guanzi/nei-ye (彼心之情，利安以寧，勿煩勿亂，和乃自成。折折乎如在於側，忽忽乎如將不得，渺渺乎如窮無極，此稽不遠，日用其德); see Rickett, trans., 40.
26. Gao Panlong, *Ru Meditation*, 19–20.
27. *Yijing, Xici shang* 繫辭上, passage 11, https://ctext.org/book-of-changes/xi-ci-shang (是故，易有太極，是生兩儀，兩儀生四象，四象生八卦，八卦定吉凶，吉凶生大業).
28. Nicholas Brasovan, *Neo-Confucian Ecological Humanism: An Interpretive Engagement with Wang Fuzhi* (1619–1692), 68.
29. Ibid., 85–6.
30. Hon, *The Yijing and Chinese Politics: Classical Commentary and Literati Activism in the Northern Song Period, 960–1127*, 14.
31. For more on this in the Chinese context, see Gardner, "Confucian Commentary and Chinese Intellectual History."

32 Ibid., 69.
33 These included Wang Bi (226–249) and Kong Yingda (574–648). See Hon, *The Yijing and Chinese Politics*, especially the second chapter.
34 Hon, *The Yijing and Chinese Politics*, 55.
35 Ibid., 53.
36 Ibid., 58–9.
37 Ibid., 76.
38 Qtd. in ibid., 93. I consulted the original at Zhang Zai 張載, *Hengqu yishuo* 橫渠易說 氣之, https://ctext.org/wiki.pl?if=gb&chapter=73915 (聚散於太虛，猶冰凝釋於水，知太虛即氣則無有無。故聖人語性與天道之極，盡於參伍之神變易而已。諸子淺妄，有有無之分，非窮理之學也). Also See Liu, *Neo-Confucianism: Metaphysics, Mind, and Morality*, 70, for a discussion of Zhang Zai's views on *qi* in this passage.
39 Hon, *The Yijing and Chinese Politics*, 90.
40 *Daxue* 大學, https://ctext.org/liji/da-xue/zh (大學之道，在明明德，在新民，在止於至善。知止而后有定，定而后能靜，靜而后能安，安而后能慮，慮而后能得。物有本末，事有終始，知所先後，則近道矣。古之欲明明德於天下者，先治其國；欲治其國者，先齊其家；欲齊其家者，先修其身；欲修其身者，先正其心；欲正其心者，先誠其意；欲誠其意者，先致其知，致知在格物。物格而後知至，知至而後意誠，意誠而後心正，心正而後身修，身修而後家齊，家齊而後國治，國治而後天下平。自天子以至於庶人，壹是皆以修身為本).
41 For more, see Ian Johston and Wang Ping, trans., *Daxue and Zhongyong*, especially Zhu's note on the text page 137.
42 Richard Wilhelm and Cary F. Baynes, trans., *The I Ching or Book of Changes*; John Blofeld, trans., *I Ching: Book of Changes*; Richard Rutt, trans., *Zhouyi: A New Translation with Commentary of the Book of Changes*.
43 Rutt, trans., *Zhouyi*, 249.
44 Rutt, trans., *Zhouyi*, 376–7. See the original at *Yijing, Daxu* 大畜, https://ctext.org/book-of-changes/da-xu (大畜，剛健篤實輝光，日新其德，剛上而尚賢。能止健，大正也。不家食吉，養賢也。利涉大川，應乎天也).

45 Qtd. in Hon, *The Yijing and Chinese Politics*, 89. From Zhang Zai 張載, *Heng qu yi shuo* 橫渠易說, passage 264, https://ctext.org/wiki.pl?if=gb&chapter=741149 (陽卦在上，而上九又在其上，故曰「剛上而尚賢」。強學者往往心多好勝，必無心處[一]之乃善也。定然後始有光明，惟能定己是光明矣，若常移易不定，何(求)來光明！易大抵以艮為止，止乃光明。時止時行，「動靜不失其時，其道光明」，「謙天道下濟而光明」，「天在山中，大畜，君子以剛健篤實輝光，日新其德」，定則自光明，故大學定而至於能慮。人心多則無由光明。[蒙雜而著著古著字雜著於物所以為蒙蒙昏蒙] 初九，有厲，利己。象曰：「有厲利己」，不犯災也). Note there is a discrepancy between the version of Zhang's text at ctext.org and Hon's translation.

46 See Hon's discussion of a Chinese "moral metaphysics" in *The Yijing and Chinese Politics*, 96; see JeeLoo Liu's article "The Is-Ought Correlation in Neo-Confucian *Qi*-Realism: How Normative Facts Exist in Natural States of *Qi*"; Donald Munro has referred to a "fact-value fusion" in Chinese thought in, for example, the essay "Unequal Human Worth"; this topic also comes up frequently in the works of well-known Chinese philosophers and sinologists Angus C. Graham, Roger T. Ames, David L. Hall, and Henry Rosemont, Jr., among others.

47 Hon, *The Yijing and Chinese Politics*, 97.

48 Zhu Xi, *Zhuzi yulei*, 性理一 (*xingliyi*), https://ctext.org/zhuzi-yulei/4. See a fuller discussion of these degrees of awareness in Zhu Xi's thought in Jana S. Rošker, *Traditional Chinese Thought and the Paradigm of Structure* (Li 理) (Cambridge: Cambridge Scholars Publishing, 2012), 132.

49 Zhu Xi, *Zhuzi yulei*, 理氣上 (*liqishang*), http://ctext.org/zhuzi-yulei/1#n586160.

50 JeeLoo Liu, *Neo-Confucianism: Metaphysics, Mind, and Morality*, 2–3.

51 JeeLoo Liu, "The Is-Ought Correlation in Neo-Confucian *Qi*-Realism," 62.

52 As Joseph Adler says in his review of the edited volume *Chinese Metaphysics and Its Problems*: "The 'problems' are not so much problems within Chinese metaphysics as they are problems in the

Western understanding of the subject." He goes on to note that the editors begin their introduction with the question, "Do the Chinese really have metaphysics?"; https://ndpr.nd.edu/news/chinese-metaphysics-and-its-problems/.

53 Hon, *The Yijing and Chinese Politics*, 96.
54 Kundera, *The Unbearable Lightness of Being*, 14.
55 Nietzsche, *The Gay Science*, 346.

Chapter 4

1 Liji 禮記, *Zhongni yanju* 仲尼燕居, passage 9, https://ctext.org/liji/zhongni-yan-ju/zh.
2 Judith Farquhar and Zhang Qicheng, *Ten Thousand Things: Nurturing Life in Contemporary Beijing*, 276.
3 Michel Foucault, "An Interview by Stephen Riggins," 131.
4 Hadot, *Philosophy as a Way of Life: Spiritual Exercises from Socrates to Foucault*, 84.
5 Ibid., 84–5.
6 Ibid., 85, 93–101.
7 Ibid., 108.
8 For example, Husserl, *Ideas Pertaining to a Pure Phenomenology and to a Phenomenological Philosophy*, and Bergson, *Matter and Memory*.
9 Bataille's experimentation with various religious and mystical practices will be discussed in the concluding chapter.
10 Parkes, *Composing the Soul*, 286–8.
11 Foulk, "Ritual in Japanese Zen Buddhism," 23.
12 Ibid.
13 For more on this subject, see my 2014 article "The Ritual Methods of Comparative Philosophy."
14 Jørn Borup, *Japanese Rinzai Zen Buddhism*, 130.
15 Ibid., 131.
16 Wong, "Editorial," 151.
17 Hori, "Teaching and Learning in the Rinzai Zen Monastery," 5.

18 Ibid., 28.
19 It is unclear to me whether we can consider Hadot's "spiritual exercises," which seem aimed at engaging the rational intellect, on a ritualistic model. For more on this question, see Bret Davis in his article "Psychomatic Practice and Kyoto School Philosophies of Zen." For more on comparisons between Hadot's spiritual exercises and Buddhist practices, see David V. Fiordalis, ed., *Buddhist Spiritual Practices: Thinking with Pierre Hadot on Buddhism, Philosophy, and the Path*.
20 Schillbrack, "Introduction: On the Use of Philosophy in the Study of Rituals," 1. One work that, in one sense, pursues such dialogue is the 2012 collection *Ritual and the Moral Life: Reclaiming the Tradition*, edited by David Solomon, Fan Ruiping, and Lo Ping-cheung. The collection marks an "interfaith" dialogue of sorts between Confucian and Christian scholars, on the moral value of ritual. The editors use a somewhat more restricted definition of ritual than the one I use in this chapter—that is, they argue intentionally *against* the sense of ritual as a broad category that can include daily habits, performative enactments, and so forth. They speak disapprovingly of the way that "relatively deritualized cosmopolitans, who[se] .... rituals are truncated, fragmented, and often misdirected (one might think of couples composing a ritual to mark their commitment to a non-marital conjugal partnership). They mark an age of moral disorientation, disengagement, cultural impoverishment and moral banality the cries out for the civilizing support of substantive rituals." See Solomon et al., "Ritual as a Cardinal Category of Moral Reality: An Introduction," 2.
21 Schillbrack, "Introduction: On the Use of Philosophy in the Study of Rituals," 1.
22 See Austin, *How to Do Things with Words*, 139. Austin's work enters religious studies via Stanley Tambiah's seminal 1979 essay "A Performative Approach to Ritual." On his influence in religious studies, see Bell, *Ritual: Perspectives and Dimensions*; Bell, *Ritual Theory, Ritual Practice*; and Ronald Grimes, *Ritual Criticism: Case Studies in Its Practice, Essays on Its Theory*.

23 Bell, *Ritual: Perspectives and Dimensions*, 69.
24 See, for example, the 2006 collection *Bodily Citations: Religion and Judith Butler* edited by Ellen Armour. For more, in general, on theoretical trends in the study of ritual efficacy, and in particular on the topic of performativity, see William S. Sax, "Ritual and the Problem of Efficacy."
25 Ames and Rosemont, "Introduction," 51.
26 Work that explores this more inclusive sense of ritual, and which invites dialogue with comparative philosophy, includes Bell's *Ritual Theory, Ritual Practice*, Ronald Grimes's *Ritual Criticism*, and Kevin Schillbrack's *Thinking through Rituals: Philosophical Perspectives*.
27 Ames and Hall, "Philosophical Introduction," 50.
28 See Sartre, *Existentialism Is a Humanism*, 20.
29 For example, Ellen Armour, ed., *Bodily Citations: Religion and Judith Butler*, which looks at Butler's work on performativity in the context of religious studies; also, Roland Faber et al., eds., *Butler on Whitehead: On the Occasion*, looking at connections between Butler's philosophy and process philosophy.
30 See Jason Ānanda Josephson, *The Invention of Religion in Japan*, and "When Buddhism Became a 'Religion': Religion and Superstition in the Writings of Inoue Enryō."
31 Heidegger, *Being and Time*, Part One, Division One, Chapter Five, section 30 "Fear as a Mode of Attunement" and Chapter Six, section 40 "The Fundamental Attunement of Anxiety as an Eminent Disclosedness of Dasein." Here I am referencing the Joan Stambaugh translation.
32 Ibid., Division Two, Chapter One, sections 46 to 53 on "being-toward-death."
33 Ibid., section 56 "The Character of Conscience as a Call."
34 Ibid., section 60 "The Existential Structure of the Authentic Potentiality-of-Being Attested to in Conscience."
35 Liji 禮記, *Tangong shang* 檀弓上, passage 9, https://ctext.org/liji/tangong-i/zh (故君子有終身之憂，而無一朝之患).
36 Ing, *The Dysfunction of Ritual in Early Confucianism*, 195.

37 *Lunyu* 論語, 9.29, https://ctext.org/analects/zh (知者不惑，仁者不憂，勇者不懼). For translations of this passage and the several that follow, I rely on Ames and Rosemont, trans., *The Analects of Confucius: A Philosophical Translation*.
38 *Lunyu*, 14.28, https://ctext.org/analects/zh (君子道者三，我無能焉：仁者不憂，知者不惑，勇者不懼).
39 *Lunyu*, 7.3, https://ctext.org/analects/zh (德之不脩，學之不講，聞義不能徙，不善不能改，是吾憂也).
40 Ing, *The Dysfunction of Ritual in Early Confucianism*, 203.
41 Ibid., 197.
42 Qtd. in Ing, *The Dysfunction of Ritual in Early Confucianism*, 195.
43 *Lunyu*, 2.6, https://ctext.org/analects/zh.
44 Legge, trans., *The Analects*, 21; Ames and Rosemont, trans., *The Analects of Confucius: A Philosophical Translation*, 77.
45 Ing, *The Dysfunction of Ritual in Early Confucianism*, 32–3.
46 Angle, "The Possibility of Sagehood: Reverence and Ethical Perfection in Zhu Xi's Thought," 286.
47 See Angle, *Sagehood*, 63–4.
48 Ibid., 86.
49 Ibid., 151.
50 And I think it goes without saying that *jing* is not grounded in the same metaphysical assumptions underlying the "spirit of seriousness" that is the subject of critique by both Beauvoir and Sartre. See, for example, Beauvoir's *Ethics of Ambiguity*, especially part II "Personal Freedom and Others."
51 Kundera, *The Unbearable Lightness of Being*, 5.
52 Ibid., 248.
53 *Daodejing* 道德經, 18, https://ctext.org/dao-de-jing/zhs.
54 *Daodejing*, 5, https://ctext.org/dao-de-jing/zhs.
55 *Daodejing*, 20, https://ctext.org/dao-de-jing/zh (荒兮其未央哉！眾人熙熙，如享太牢，如春登臺。我獨怕兮其未兆；如嬰兒之未孩；儽儽兮若無所歸). I consulted Ivanhoe, trans., "Laozi ('*The Daodejing*')," 172; and Ames and Hall, trans., *Daodejing*, 105–6.

56 *Daodejing*, 10, https://ctext.org/dao-de-jing/zh (生之、畜之，生而不有，為而不恃，長而不宰，是謂玄德). I consulted Ivanhoe, trans., "Laozi ('*The Daodejing*')," 167; and Ames and Hall, trans., *Daodejing*, 90.
57 Ames and Hall, trans., *Daodejing*, 90–1.
58 This is to borrow Tze-Ki Hon's phrase from the last chapter. See Hon, *The Yijing and Chinese Politics*, 96.
59 Sartre, *Being and Nothingness*, 22.
60 Fiona Ellis, "Sartre on Mind and World," 32–3.
61 Ibid., 43–4.
62 Ames and Hall, "Introduction: A Philosophical Interpretation of the *Zhongyong*," 12.
63 Ibid., 12, 13.
64 Ibid., 13.
65 Ibid., 32.
66 For a different take on some of the issues I discuss in this section, in reference to Daoist philosophy, see Paul J. D'Ambrosio, "Authenticity in the *Zhuangzi*? Contemporary Misreadings of '*Zhen*' 真 and an Alternative to Existentialism."
67 Heidegger, *Being and Time*, especially Division Two, Chapter One.
68 Ibid., especially Division One, Chapter Five, sections 35–38.
69 I.e., Beauvoir's *Ethics of Ambiguity*.
70 *Daxue* 大學, https://ctext.org/liji/da-xue/zh. I consulted Ian Johnston and Wang Ping, trans., *Daxue and Zhongyong*, 135.
71 Johnston and Wang, trans., *Daxue and Zhongyong*, 49.
72 Ibid., 139.
73 Ibid.
74 See Adler, "*Shen* in Neo-Confucian Discourse," 133. For more on this, see Kim Yung-Sik, "'Analogical Extension' (*leitui*) in Zhu Xi's Methodology of 'Investigation of Things' (*gewu*) and 'Extension of Knowledge' (*zhizhi*)." Though Kim's focus is on the method of analogical extension, as more or less a method of reasoning, he also notes the phenomenon of "a kind of 'resonance' between the mind's *li* and the things' *li*," which, as he comments, is "not primarily an intellectual process" (39).

75 Qtd. in ibid., 125.
76 Ibid., 132.
77 Ibid., 141. Bracketed material is mine.
78 Johnston and Wang, trans., *Daxue and Zhongyong*., 325.
79 Ibid., 324–5.
80 Ibid., 337.
81 Ibid.
82 See Graham, trans., *Chuang-tzu: The Inner Chapter*, 63–4.
83 Ibid., 135, 138.
84 Hiraga, "*Tao* of Learning: Metaphors Japanese Students Live By," 62–3.
85 Bradley Park, "Vitality as Responsivity: Levinas and Lao-Zhuang Daoism," 221.
86 See, for example, Roger T. Ames, "Nietzsche's 'Will to Power' and Chinese 'Virtuality' (*De*): A Comparative Study"; Bret Davis "Zen after Zarathustra: The Problem of the Will in the Confrontation between Nietzsche and Buddhism," and "Reply to Graham Parkes: Nietzsche as Zebra: With both Egoistic Antibuddha and Nonegoistic Bodhisattva Stripes"; Graham Parkes, "Open Letter to Bret Davis—Letter on Egoism: Will to Power as Interpretation," and "Response to Bret Davis—Zarathustra and Asian Thought: A Few Final Words"; and most recently Jason Wirth in *Nietzsche and Other Buddhas*.
87 Angle, *Sagehood*, Chapter 7 "Sagely Ease and Moral Perception."
88 See Jin Y. Park, *Women and Buddhist Philosophy: Engaging Zen Master Kim Iryŏp*, 66–72.
89 For example, Edward T. Ch'ien, "The Neo-Confucian Confrontation with Buddhism: A Structural and Historical Analysis"; or Robert H. Sharf, "The Buddha's Finger Bones and the Art of Chinese Esoteric Buddhism."
90 See Albert Welter, *The Administration of Buddhism in China: A Study and Translation of Zanning and His Topical Compendium of the Buddhist Order in China*; also Daniel Getz, "A Confucian Pure Land? Longshu's Treatise on Pure Land by Wang Rixiu." For more on the Korean context see Boudewijn Walraven, "Buddhist Accommodation and Appropriation and the Limits of Confucianization"; and Jongmyung Kim, "Kings and Buddhism in Medieval Korea."

91 Bongkil Chung, "Won Buddhism: A Synthesis of the Moral Systems of Confucianism and Buddhism."
92 See Parkes, "Nietzsche, Panpsychism, and Pure Experience: An East Asian Contemplative Perspective," and "Nietzsche's Care for Stone: The Dead, Dance, and Flying."
93 *Daxue* 大學, https://ctext.org/liji/da-xue/zh.

Conclusion

1 Bataille, *On Nietzsche*, 49.
2 Ibid., 22.
3 Kim Iryŏp, *Reflections of a Zen Buddhist Nun*, 41.
4 Various biographical works on Bataille are available. Perhaps the most scandalous charge against him concerns the Acéphale society and its purported aspiration to carry out human sacrifice. See, for example, Leslie Hill, *Nancy, Blanchot: A Serious Controversy*, 23–24.
5 Leslie Hill, *Nancy, Blanchot: A Serious Controversy*, 133.
6 Bataille, *Inner Experience*, 94.
7 Ibid., 112.
8 Zhu Xi, *Daxue zhangju*, passage 6, https://ctext.org/si-shu-zhang-ju-ji-zhu/da-xue-zhang-ju (至於用力之久，而一旦豁然貫通焉，則眾物之表裏精粗無不到，而吾心之全體大用無不明矣). See also Adler, "Varieties of Spiritual Experience: *Shen* in Neo-Confucian Discourse," 134.
9 Adler, "Varieties of Spiritual Experience," 134.
10 Bataille, *Inner Experience*, 114.
11 Bataille, *On Nietzsche*, 22.
12 Ibid., 39.
13 Surkis, "No Fun and Games until Someone Loses an Eye: Transgression and Masculinity in Bataille and Foucault," 19.
14 Foucault, "A Preface to Transgression," 34–5.
15 Liu, "Was There Something in Nothingness? The Debate on the Primordial State between Daoism and Neo-Confucianism," 181.
16 Kaibara Ekken, *The Philosophy of Qi: The Record of Great Doubts*, 128.

17 Kaibara Ekiken, *Taigiroku* 大疑録, 166-7. The above translation, with modification, from Mary Evelyn Tucker's version in Kaibara Ekken, *The Philosophy of Qi: The Record of Great Doubts*, 128. For consistency, I have used *pinyin* pronunciation, since Ekken was writing in literary Chinese.

18 As Ekken certainly would have known, Zhu Xi wrote his own polemics against Buddhist thought. See Chu Hsi and Lü Tsu-Ch'ien [Zhu Xi and Lü Zuqian], *Reflections on Things at Hand*, "Sifting the Heterodoxical Doctrines," 279–88.

19 For some discussion of this, see Matteo Cestari, "Between Emptiness and Absolute Nothingness: Reflections on Negation in Nishida and Buddhism," 328. For an extended overview of Chinese translators' attempts to deal with Sanskrit Buddhist terms vis-à-vis Daoist and Ruist terminology (especially on the issue of translating *śūnyatā* and other key concepts in Mahāyāna thought), see Sarah Mattice, *Emptying and Forming: A Philosophical Translation and Commentary on the Heart Sutra*.

20 Ibid., 191.

21 Heidegger, *Being and Time*, 282 (Macquerrie and Robinson translation).

22 Kopf, "When Expression Is Expressed, Non-Expression Is Not Expressed: A Zen Buddhist Approach to Talking about the Ineffable," 146.

23 Henry Rosemont, Jr., "Is There a Universal Path of Spiritual Progress in the Texts of Early Confucianism?" 192 and 195, n14.

24 Zhu Xi, qtd. in Stephen C. Angle, *Sagehood*, 144.

25 Angle, *Sagehood*, 140–4.

26 Ibid., 177–8. Parenthetical material is in the original; bracketed material is mine.

27 Zhu Xi, *Zhuzi Yulei*, 學四 (*xuesi*), passage 24; https://ctext.org/zhuzi-yulei/10 (須是一棒一條痕！一摑一掌血！看人文字，要當如此，豈可忽略！). See also Chu Hsi [Zhu Xi], *Learning to Be a Sage*, 130.

28 Bataille, *Inner Experience*, 94.

29 Tu Wei-ming, "'Inner Experience': The Basis of Creativity in Neo-Confucian Thinking," in *Humanity and Self-Cultivation*, 102–10. The original version of the article appears in Christian F. Murck, ed., *Artists and Traditions: Uses of the Past in Chinese Culture*, 9–15 (Princeton: The Art Museum, Princeton University, 1976).
30 Ibid., 106–7.
31 Ibid., 108.
32 Hadot, *Philosophy as a Way of Life*, 108–9. He is referencing the essayist Vauvenargues.

References

Adamek, Wendi. *Mystique of Transmission: On Early Chan History and Its Contexts*. New York: Columbia University Press, 2017.

Adler, Joseph A. "Review of *Chinese Metaphysics and Its Problems*." *Notre Dame Philosophical Reviews* (July 17, 2015). https://ndpr.nd.edu/news/chinese-metaphysics-and-its-problems/. Accessed September 2, 2019.

Adler, Joseph A. "Varieties of Spiritual Experience: *Shen* in Neo-Confucian Discourse." In *Confucian Spirituality*, Vol. 2, edited by Tu Wei-ming and Mary Evelyn Tucker, 120–48. New York: Crossroad, 2004.

Ames, Roger T. "Nietzsche's 'Will to Power' and Chinese 'Virtuality' (*De*): A Comparative Study." In *Nietzsche and Asian Thought*, edited by Graham Parkes, 130–50. Chicago: Chicago University Press, 1991.

Ames, Roger T., and David L. Hall, trans. *Daodejing "Making This Life Significant": A Philosophical Translation*. New York: Ballantine Books, 2003.

Ames, Roger T., and David L. Hall. *Focusing the Familiar: A Translation and Philosophical Interpretation of the* Zhongyong. Honolulu: University of Hawai'i Press, 2001.

Ames, Roger T., and David L. Hall. "Introduction: A Philosophical Interpretation of the *Zhongyong*." In *Focusing the Familiar: A Translation and Philosophical Interpretation of the* Zhongyong, translated by Roger T. Ames and David L. Hall, 1–60. Honolulu: University of Hawai'i Press, 2001.

Ames, Roger T., and Henry Rosemont, Jr. "Introduction." In *The Analects of Confucius: A Philosophical Translation*, translated by Ames and Rosemont, 1–70. New York: Ballantine Books, 1998.

Ames, Roger T., and Henry Rosemont, Jr., trans. *The Analects of Confucius: A Philosophical Translation*. New York: Random House, 1998.

Angle, Stephen C. "The Possibility of Sagehood: Reverence and Ethical Perfection in Zhu Xi's Thought." *Journal of Chinese Philosophy* 25, no. 3 (September 1988): 281–303.

Angle, Stephen C. *Sagehood: The Contemporary Significance of Neo-Confucian Philosophy*. Oxford: Oxford University Press, 2009.

Angle, Stephen C. "*Tian* as Cosmos in Zhu Xi's Neo-Confucianism." *Dao* 17 (2008): 169–85.

Angle, Stephen C., and Justin Tiwald. *Neo-Confucianism: A Philosophical Introduction*. Cambridge: Polity Press, 2017.

Armour, Ellen, ed. *Bodily Citations: Religion and Judith Butler*. New York: Columbia University Press, 2006.

Aquinas. *Questiones Disputatae de Veritate*. Priory of the Immaculate Conception at the Dominican House of Studies. https://dhspriory.org/thomas/QDdeVer1.htm. Accessed August 31, 2019.

Austin, J. L. *How to Do Things with Words*. Edited by J. O. Urmson and Marina Sbisá. Cambridge: Harvard University Press, 1962.

Baba, Eiho. "*Zhijue* as Appreciation and Realization in Zhu Xi: An Examination through Hun and Po." *Philosophy East and West* 67, no. 2 (April 2017): 301–17.

Bao, Jiemin. "Merit-Making: Capitalism Re-territorializing Thai Buddhism in Silicon Valley, California." *Journal of Asian American Studies* 8, no. 2 (2005): 115–42.

Bataille, Georges. *Inner Experience*. Translated by Leslie Anne Boldt. Albany: SUNY Press, 1988.

Bataille, Georges. *On Nietzsche*. Translated by Bruce Boone. London: Continuum, 2004.

Beauvoir, Simone de. *Ethics of Ambiguity*. Translated by B. Frechtman. New York: Citadel Press, 1976.

Bell Catherine. *Ritual: Perspectives and Dimensions*. Oxford: Oxford University Press, 1997, rev. 2009.

Bell Catherine. *Ritual Theory, Ritual Practice*. Oxford: Oxford University Press, 1992.

Bergson, Henri. *Matter and Memory*. Translated by N. M. Paul and W. S. Palmer. New York: Zone Books, 1990.

Berkeley, George. *A Treatise Concerning the Principles of Human Knowledge*. Edited by Kenneth Winkler. Indianapolis: Hackett: 1982.

Blackburn, Simon. *The Oxford Dictionary of Philosophy*. Revised second edition. Oxford: Oxford University Press, 2008.

Blofeld, John, trans. *I Ching: Book of Changes*. New York: Compass, 1965.

Bodhi, Bhikkhu, ed. *In the Buddha's Words*. Somerville, MA: Wisdom, 2005.

Borup, Jørn. *Japanese Rinzai Zen Buddhism: Myōshinji, a Living Religion.* Leiden: Brill, 2008.

Brasovan, Nicholas. *Neo-Confucian Ecological Humanism: An Interpretive Engagement with Wang Fuzhi (1619–1692).* Albany: State University of New York Press, 2017.

Butler, Judith. *Gender Trouble: Feminism and the Subversion of Identity.* New York: Routledge, 1999.

Cahn, Steven M. "Meaningless Lives?" In *The Meaning of Life: A Reader*, edited by E. D. Klemke and Steven M. Cahn, 236–7. New York: Oxford University Press, 2008.

Cestari, Matteo. "Between Emptiness and Absolute Nothingness: Reflections on Negation in Nishida and Buddhism." In *Frontiers of Japanese Philosophy: Japanese Philosophy Abroad*, edited by James W. Heisig and Rein Raud, 320–46. Nagoya: Nanzan Institute for Religion and Culture, 2010.

Chiavetta, Christopher. *Green Key.* 2019. Acrylic on paper, 12 by 12 in. West Des Moines, Olson-Larsen Galleries.

Ch'ien, Edward T. "The Neo-Confucian Confrontation with Buddhism: A Structural and Historical Analysis." *Journal of Chinese Philosophy* 15 (1988): 347–69.

Chu Hsi [Zhu Xi]. *Learning to Be a Sage: Selection from the Conversations of Master Chu, Arranged Topically.* Translated by Daniel K. Gardner. Berkeley: University of California Press, 1990.

Chu Hsi and Lü Tsu-Ch'ien [Zhu Xi and Lü Zuqian]. *Reflections on Things at Hand.* Translated by Wing-Tsit Chan. New York and London: Columbia University Press, 1967.

Chung, Bongkil. "Won Buddhism: A Synthesis of the Moral Systems of Confucianism and Buddhism." *Journal of Chinese Philosophy* 15 (1988): 425–48.

Clark, Maudemarie. "Nietzsche and Value Creation." *Nietzsche-Studien* 44, no. 1 (2015): 98–103.

Clark, Maudemarie and David Dudrick. "Nietzsche and Moral Objectivity: The Development of Nietzsche's Metaethics." In *Nietzsche and Morality*, edited by Neil Sinhababu and Brian Leiter, 192–226. Oxford: Oxford University Press, 2007.

Cleary, Thomas, trans. *The Sutra of Hui-neng.* Boston: Shambhala, 1998.

Curley, Melissa Anne-Marie. *Pure Land/Real World: Modern Buddhism, Japanese Leftists, and the Utopian Imagination*. Honolulu: University of Hawai'i Press, 2017.

D'Ambrosio, Paul J. "Authenticity in the *Zhuangzi*? Contemporary Misreadings of '*Zhen*' 真 and an Alternative to Existentialism." *Frontiers of Philosophy in China* 10, 3 (2015): 353–79.

Daodejing 道德經. In *Chinese Text Project*, edited by Donald Sturgeon. 2011. https://ctext.org/dao-de-jing/zhs.

Davis, Bret W. "Psychomatic Practice and Kyoto School Philosophies of Zen." *Journal of Religious Philosophy* 64 (2013): 25–48.

Davis, Bret W. "Reply to Graham Parkes: Nietzsche as Zebra: With both Egoistic Antibuddha and Nonegoistic Bodhisattva Stripes." *Journal of Nietzsche Studies*, 46, no. 1 (Spring 2015): 62–81.

Davis, Bret W. "Zen after Zarathustra: The Problem of the Will in the Confrontation between Nietzsche and Buddhism." *Journal of Nietzsche Studies*, no. 28 (Autumn 2004): 89–138.

Daxue 大學. In *Chinese Text Project*, edited by Donald Sturgeon. 2011. https://ctext.org/liji/da-xue/zh.

Descartes, René. *Meditations on First Philosophy (with Selections from the Objections and Replies)*. Translated and edited by John Cottingham. Second edition. Cambridge: Cambridge University Press, 2017.

Dries, Manuel. "How Hard Is It to Create Values?" *Nietzsche-Studien* 44, no. 1 (2015): 30–43.

Ellis, Fiona. "Sartre on Mind and World." *Sartre Studies International* 6, no. 1 (2000): 23–47.

Faber, Roland, Michael Halewood, and Deena M. Lin, eds. *Butler on Whitehead: On the Occasion*. Lanham: Lexington, 2012.

Farquhar, Judith, and Zhang Qicheng. *Ten Thousand Things: Nurturing Life in Contemporary Beijing*. New York: Zone Books, 2012.

Fiordalis, David V., ed. *Buddhist Spiritual Practices: Thinking with Pierre Hadot on Buddhism, Philosophy, and the Path*. Berkeley: Mangalam Press, 2019.

Flanagan, Owen. *The Really Hard Problem: Meaning in a Material World*. Cambridge: MIT Press, 2007.

Foucault, Michel. "An Interview by Stephen Riggins." In *Ethics: Subjectivity and Truth*, edited by Paul Rabinow, 121–34. New York: The New Press, 1997.

Foucault, Michel. "A Preface to Transgression." In *Language, Counter-Memory, Practice: Selected Essays and Interviews*, edited by Donald F. Bouchard, translated by Bouchard and Sherry Simon, 29–52. Ithaca: Cornell University Press, 1977.

Foucault, Michel. "Technologies of the Self." In *Technologies of the Self: A Seminar with Michel Foucault*, edited by Luther H. Martin, Huck Gutman, and Patrick H. Hutton, 16–49. Amherst: University of Massachusetts Press, 1988.

Foulk, Griffith T. "Ritual in Japanese Zen Buddhism." In *Zen Ritual: Studies of Zen Buddhist Theory in Practice*, edited by, S. Heine and D. S. Wright, 21–82. Oxford: Oxford University Press, 2008.

Gadamer, Hans-Georg. *Truth and Method*. Translated revised by Joel Weinsheimer and Donald G. Marshall. London: Bloomsbury, 2013.

Gao Panlong. *Ru Meditation: Gao Panlong (1562–1626 CE)*. Translated by Bin Song. Edited by Paul Blair. Boston: Ru Media Company, 2018.

Gardner, Daniel K. "Confucian Commentary Chinese Intellectual History." *Journal of Asian Studies* 57, no. 2 (1998): 397–422.

Gardner, Daniel K., trans. *Learning to Be a Sage: Selection from the Conversations of Master Chu, Arranged Topically*, by Chu Hsi [Zhu Xi]. Berkeley: University of California Press, 1990.

Getz, Daniel. "A Confucian Pure Land? Longshu's Treatise on Pure Land by Wang Rixiu." In *Pure Lands in Asian Texts and Contexts: An Anthology*, edited by Georgios T. Halkias and Richard K. Payne, 602–30. Honolulu: University of Hawai'i Press, 2019.

Godart, Gerard Clinton. "'Philosophy' or 'Religion'? The Confrontation with Foreign Categories in Late Nineteenth Century Japan." *Journal of the History of Ideas* 69, no. 1 (2008): 71–91.

Goff, Philip. *Galileo's Error: Foundations for a New Science of Consciousness*. New York: Pantheon, 2019.

Graham, A. C., trans. *Chuang-tzu: The Inner Chapters*. Indianapolis: Hackett, 1981.

Gregg, Nina. "Reflections on the Feminist Critique of Objectivity." *Journal of Communication Inquiry* 11, no. 1 (1987): 8–18.

Grimes, Ronald. *Ritual Criticism: Case Studies in Its Practice, Essays on Its Theory*. Columbia: University of South Carolina Press, 1990.

Guanzi 管子. *Jie* 戒. In *Chinese Text Project*, edited by Donald Sturgeon. 2011. https://ctext.org/guanzi/jie.

Guanzi 管子. *Neiye* 內業. In *Chinese Text Project*, edited by Donald Sturgeon. 2011. http://ctext.org/guanzi/nei-ye.

Guanzi 管子. *Xinshu xia*" 心術下. In *Chinese Text Project*, edited by Donald Sturgeon. 2011. https://ctext.org/guanzi/xin-shu-ii.

Hadot, Pierre. *Philosophy as a Way of Life: Spiritual Exercises from Socrates to Foucault*. Edited by Arnold I. Davidson. Translated by Michael Chase. Oxford: Blackwell, 1995.

Heidegger, Martin. *Being and Time*. Translated by John Macquarrie and Edward Robinson. New York: HarperCollins, 2008.

Heidegger, Martin. *Being and Time*. Translated by Joan Stambaugh. Revised by Dennis J. Schmidt. Albany: SUNY Press, 2010.

Hill, Leslie. *Nancy, Blanchot: A Serious Controversy*. London: Rowman & Littlefield International, 2018.

Hiraga, Masako K. "*Tao* of Learning: Metaphors Japanese Students Live by." In *Metaphors for Education: A Cross-Cultural Perspective*, edited by Erich Berendt, 55–72. Amsterdam: John Benjamins, 2008.

Hobbes, Thomas. *Elements of Law: Natural and Political*. Edited by J. C. A. Gaskin. Oxford: Oxford University Press, 1994.

Holder, John J., ed. and trans. *Early Buddhist Discourses*. Indianapolis: Hackett, 2006.

Hon, Tze-Ki. *The Yijing and Chinese Politics: Classical Commentary and Literati Activism in the Northern Song Period, 960–1127*. Abany: State University of New York Press, 2005.

Hori, G. Victor Sōgen. "Teaching and Learning in the Rinzai Zen Monastery." *Journal of Japanese Studies* 20, no. 1 (1994): 5–35.

Hubbard, Jamie. *Absolute Delusion, Perfect Buddhahood: The Rise and Fall of a Chinese Heresy*. Honolulu: University of Hawai'i Press, 2001.

Huineng 惠能. *Bore* 般若 [Prajñā]. *Liuzutanjing* 六祖壇經. In *Chinese Text Project*, edited by Donald Sturgeon. 2011. https://ctext.org/wiki.pl?if=gb&chapter=459983.

Huddleston, Andrew. "Nietzsche's Meta-Axiology: Against the Sceptical Readings." *British Journal for the History of Philosophy* 22, no. 2 (2014): 322–42.

Hume, David. *An Enquiry Concerning Human Understanding*. Edited by Tom L. Beauchamp. Oxford: Oxford University Press, 1999.

Hume, David. *Treatise of Human Nature*. Edited by L. A. Selby-Bigge and P. H. Nidditch. Oxford: Oxford University Press, 1978.

Hussain, Nadeem. "Honest Illusion: Valuing for Nietzsche's Free Spirits." In *Nietzsche and Morality*, edited by Neil Sinhababu and Brian Leiter, 157–91. Oxford: Oxford University Press, 2007.

Husserl, Edmund. *Ideas Pertaining to a Pure Phenomenology and to a Phenomenological Philosophy—First Book: General Introduction to a Pure Phenomenology*. Translated by F. Kersten. The Hague: Nijhoff, 1982.

Ing, Michael. *The Dysfunction of Ritual in Early Confucianism*. Oxford: Oxford University Press, 2012.

Ivanoe, Philip J., trans. "Laozi ('*The Daodejing*')." In *Readings in Classical Chinese Philosophy*, edited by Philip J. Ivanhoe and Bryan W. Van Norden, 161–205. Indianapolis: Hackett, 2001.

Ivanoe, Philip J. *Readings from the Lu-Wang School of Neo-Confucianism*. Indianapolis: Hackett, 2009.

Ivanhoe, Philip J. *Three Streams: Confucian Reflections on Learning and the Moral Heart-Mind in China, Korea, and Japan*. Oxford: Oxford University Press, 2016.

Johnston, Ian, and Wang Ping, trans. *Daxue and Zhongyong: Bilingual Edition*. Hong Kong: The Chinese University Press, 2012.

Josephson, Jason Ānanda. *The Invention of Religion in Japan*. Chicago: University of Chicago Press, 2012.

Josephson, Jason Ānanda. "When Buddhism Became a 'Religion': Religion and Superstition in the Writings of Inoue Enryō." *Japanese Journal of Religious Studies* 33, no. 1 (2006): 143–68.

Kaibara Ekken [also Ekiken]. *The Philosophy of Qi: The Record of Great Doubts*. Translated by Mary Evelyn Tucker. New York: Columbia University Press, 2007.

Kaibara Ekiken [also Ekken] 貝原益軒. *Taigiroku* 大疑録. In *Ekiken zenshū* 益軒全集, Vol. 2, 148–75. Tokyo: Kaibara Ekiken Kankōbu, 1910.

Kalmanson, Leah. "Dharma and Dao: Key Terms in the Comparative Philosophy of Religion." In *Ineffability: An Exercise in Comparative Philosophy of Religion*, edited by Tim Knepper and Leah Kalmanson, 245–55. Cham, Switzerland: Springer, 2017.

Kalmanson, Leah. "The Ritual Methods of Comparative Philosophy." *Philosophy East and West* 67, no. 2 (2017): 399–418.

Kant, Immanuel. *Critique of Pure Reason*. Translated and edited by Paul Guyer and Allen W. Wood. Cambridge: Cambridge University Press, 1998.

Kasulis, Thomas P. *Engaging Japanese Philosophy: A Short History*. Honolulu: University of Hawai'i Press, 2018.

Kim Iryŏp. 2014. *Reflections of a Zen Buddhist Nun*. Translated by Jin Y. Park. Honolulu: University of Hawai'i Press.

Kim Jongmyung. "Kings and Buddhism in Medieval Korea." *Korean Studies* 41 (2007): 128–51.

Kim Yung Sik. "'Analogical Extension' (*leitui*) in Zhu Xi's Methodology of 'Investigation of Things' (*gewu*) and 'Extension of Knowledge' (*zhizhi*)." In *Questioning Science in East Asian Contexts: Essays on Science, Confucianism, and the Comparative History of Science*, edited by Kim Yung Sik, 35–52. Leiden: Brill, 2014.

Kim Yung Sik. "Zhu Xi on Scientific and Occult Subjects: Defining and Extending the Boundaries of Confucian Learning." In *Returning to Zhu Xi: Emerging Patterns within the Supreme Polarity*, edited by David Jones and Jinli He, 121–46. Albany: SUNY Press, 2015.

Kopf, Gereon. "When Expression Is Expressed, Non-Expression Is Not Expressed: A Zen Buddhist Approach to Talking about the Ineffable." In *Ineffability: An Exercise in Comparative Philosophy of Religion*, edited by Timothy D. Knepper and Leah E. Kalmanson, 135–56. Cham, Switzerland: Springer, 2017.

Kundera, Milan. *Immortality*. Translated by Peter Kussi. New York: Perennial Classics, 1999.

Kundera, Milan. *The Unbearable Lightness of Being*. Translated by Michael Henry Heim. New York: Perennial Classics, 1999.

Langsam, Harold. "Nietzsche and Value Creation: Subjectivism, Self-Expression, and Strength." *Inquiry* 61, no. 1 (2018): 100–13.

Lazzarato, Maurizio. *Signs and Machines: Capitalism and the Production of Subjectivity*. Los Angeles: Semiotext(e), 2014.

Lee, Jae-Yon. "Authors as Creators of Art: The Collaborative Shaping of Literary Writers in *Ch'angjo*." *The Journal of Korean Studies* 20, no. 1 (Spring 2015): 77–112.

Legge, James, trans. *The Analects*. By Confucius. Digireads.com, 2017.

Li, Chenyang, and Franklin Perkins, eds. *Chinese Metaphysics and Its Problems*. Cambridge: Cambridge University Press, 2015.

Liji 禮記. *Tangong shang* 檀弓上. In *Chinese Text Project*, edited by Donald Sturgeon. 2011. https://ctext.org/liji/tan-gong-i/zh.

Liji 禮記. *Zhongni yanju* 仲尼燕居. In *Chinese Text Project*, edited by Donald Sturgeon. 2011. https://ctext.org/liji/zhongni-yan-ju/zh.

Liu, JeeLoo. "Chinese *Qi*-Naturalism and Liberal Naturalism." *Philosophy, Theology, and the Sciences* 1, no. 1 (2014): 59–86.

Liu, JeeLoo. "The Is-Ought Correlation in Neo-Confucian *Qi*-Realism: How Normative Facts Exist in Natural States of *Qi*." *Contemporary Chinese Thought* 42, no. 1 (Fall 2011): 60–77.

Liu, JeeLoo. *Neo-Confucianism: Metaphysics, Mind, and Morality*. Malden, MA: Wiley, 2018.

Liu, JeeLoo. "Was There Something in Nothingness? The Debate on the Primordial State between Daoism and Neo-Confucianism." In *Nothingness in Asian Philosophy*, edited by JeeLoo Liu and Douglas L. Berger, 181–96. New York: Routledge, 2014.

Locke, John. *An Essay Concerning Human Understanding*. Edited by Kenneth P. Winkler. Indianapolis: Hackett, 1996.

Lunyu 論語. In *Chinese Text Project*, edited by Donald Sturgeon. 2011. https://ctext.org/analects/zh.

Mackenzie, Catriona, and Natalie Stoljar, eds. *Relational Autonomy: Feminist Perspectives on Autonomy, Agency, and the Social Self*. Oxford: Oxford University Press, 2000.

Mattice, Sarah. *Emptying and Forming: A Philosophical Translation and Commentary on the Heart Sutra*. Lexington Books, Under contract.

Meillassoux, Quentin. *After Finitude: An Essay on the Necessity of Contingency*. Translated by Ray Brassier. London: Continuum, 2008.

Merleau-Ponty, Maurice. *Phenomenology of Perception*. Translated by Donald Landes. London: Routledge, 2012.

Miller, James. *China's Green Religion: Daoism and the Quest for a Sustainable Future*. New York: Columbia University Press, 2017.

Miller, James. "Daoism and Nature." In *Nature across Cultures: Views of Nature and the Environment in Non-Western Cultures*, edited by Helaine Selin, 393–409. Dordrecht: Springer, 2003.

Munro, Donald J. "Unequal Human Worth." In *The Philosophical Challenge from China*, edited by Brian Bruya, 121–58. Cambridge: MIT Press, 2015.

Nelson, Eric S. "Kim Iryŏp's Existential Buddhism: Book Review of Jin Y. Park, trans. and introduction, *Reflections of a Zen Buddhist Nun: Essays by Zen Master Kim Iryŏp.*" *Philosophy East and West* 66, no. 3 (July 2016): 1049–51.

Nietzsche, Friedrich. *Beyond Good and Evil*. Translated by Walter Kaufmann. New York: Vintage, 1966.

Nietzsche, Friedrich. *The Gay Science*. Translated by Walter Kaufmann. New York: Vintage, 1974.

Nietzsche, Friedrich. *On the Genealogy of Morality*. Translated by Maudemarie Clark and Alan Swensen. Indianapolis: Hackett, 1998.

Nietzsche, Friedrich. *Thus Spoke Zarathustra: A Book for Everyone and Nobody*. Translated by Graham Parkes. Oxford: Oxford University Press, 2008.

Nishitani Keiji. *The Self-Overcoming of Nihilism*. Translated by Graham Parkes and Setsuko Aihara. Albany: SUNY Press, 1990.

Park, Bradley. "Vitality as Responsivity: Levinas and Lao-Zhuang Daoism." In *Levinas and Asian Thought*, edited by Leah Kalmanson, Frank Garrett, and Sarah Mattice. Pittsburgh: Duquesne University Press, 2014.

Park, Jin Y. "Translator's Introduction: Kim Iryŏp, Her Life and Thought." In *Reflections of a Zen Buddhist Nun*, by Kim Iryop, translated by Jin Y. Park, 1–26. Honolulu: University of Hawai'i Press, 2014.

Park, Jin Y. *Women and Buddhist Philosophy: Engaging Zen Master Kim Iryŏp*. Honolulu: University of Hawai'i Press, 2017.

Parkes, Graham. *Composing the Soul: Reaches of Nietzsche's Psychology*. Chicago: University of Chicago Press, 1994.

Parkes, Graham, ed. *Heidegger and Asian Thought*. Honolulu: University of Hawai'i Press, 1987.

Parkes, Graham. *Nietzsche and Asian Thought*. Chicago: University of Chicago Press, 1991.

Parkes, Graham. "Nietzsche's Care for Stone: The Dead, Dance, and Flying." In *Nietzsche's Therapeutic Teaching for Individuals and Culture*, edited by Horst Hutter and Eli Friedland, 175–90. London: Bloomsbury, 2013.

Parkes, Graham. "Nietzsche, Panpsychism, and Pure Experience: An East Asian Contemplative Perspective." In *Nietzsche and Phenomenology*, edited by Andrea Rehberg, 87–100. Newcastle upon Tyne: Cambridge Scholars Publishing, 2011.

Parkes, Graham. "Open Letter to Bret Davis—Letter on Egoism: Will to Power as Interpretation." *Journal of Nietzsche Studies* 46, no. 1 (Spring 2015): 42–61.

Parkes, Graham. "Response to Bret Davis—Zarathustra and Asian Thought: A Few Final Words." *Journal of Nietzsche Studies* 46, no. 1 (Spring 2015): 82–8.

Parkes, Graham. "Winds, Waters, and Earth Energies: *Fengshui* and Awareness of Place." In *Nature across Cultures: Views of Nature and the Environment in Non-Western Cultures*, edited by Helaine Selin, 185–209. Dordrecht: Springer, 2003.

Pattison, George, and Kate Kirkpatrick, eds. *The Mystical Sources of Existentialist Thought: Being, Nothingness, Love*. New York: Routledge, 2019.

Poellner, Peter. "Affect, Value, and Objectivity." In *Nietzsche and Morality*, edited by Neil Sinhababu and Brian Leiter, 227–61. Oxford: Oxford University Press, 2007.

Rickett, W. Allyn, trans. *Guanzi: Political, Economic, and Philosophical Essays from Early China*, Vols. 1 and 2. Princeton: Princeton University Press, 1998.

Rosemont Jr., Henry. "Is There a Universal Path of Spiritual Progress in the Texts of Early Confucianism." In *Confucian Spirituality*, Vol. 2, edited by Tu Wei-ming and Mary Evelyn Tucker, 183–96. New York: Crossroad, 2004.

Rošker, Jana S. *Traditional Chinese Thought and the Paradigm of Structure* (Li 理). Cambridge: Cambridge Scholars Publishing, 2012.

Rowell, Teresina. *The Background and Early Use of the Buddha-Kṣetra Concept*. Introduction and Chapter One. *The Eastern Buddhist*, Vol. 6–3 (1934): 199–246.

Rutt, Richard, trans. *Zhouyi: A New Translation with Commentary of the Book of Changes*. London: RoutledgeCurzon, 2002.

Sartre, Jean-Paul. *Being and Nothingness: An Essay in Phenomenological Ontology*. Translated by Hazel E. Barnes. New York: Citadel Press, 1956.

Sartre, Jean-Paul. *Existentialism Is a Humanism*. Translated by Carol Macomber. New Haven: Yale University Press, 2007.

Sax, William S. "Ritual and the Problem of Efficacy." In *The Problem of Ritual Efficacy*, edited by William S. Sax, Johannes Quack, and Jan Weinhold, 3–16. Oxford: Oxford University Press, 2010.

Sharf, Robert H. "The Buddha's Finger Bones and the Art of Chinese Esoteric Buddhism." *The Art Bulletin* 93, no. 1 (March 2011): 38–59.

Sharf, Robert H. *Coming to Terms with Chinese Buddhism: A Reading of the Treasure Store Treatise*. Honolulu: University of Hawai'i Press, 2002.

Shaviro, Steven. *Without Criteria: Kant, Whitehead, Deleuze, and Aesthetics*. Cambridge: MIT Press, 2009.

Shillbrack, Kevin. "Introduction: On the Use of Philosophy in the Study of Rituals." In *Thinking through Rituals: Philosophical Perspectives*, edited by Kevin Schillbrack, 1–30. New York: Routledge, 2004.

Shinran. *The Collected Works of Shinran, Volume 1: The Writings*. Translated by Dennis Hirota et al. Kyoto: Jōdo Shinshū Hongwanji-ha, 1997.

Silk, Alex. "Nietzschean Constructivism: Ethics and Metaethics for All and None." *Inquiry* 58, no. 3 (2015): 244–80.

Sinhababu, Neil, and Brian Leiter, eds. *Nietzsche and Morality*. Oxford: Oxford University Press, 2007.

Solomon, David, Ruiping Fan, Ping-cheung Lo, and H. Tristram Engelhardt, Jr. "Ritual as a Cardinal Category of Moral Reality: An Introduction." In *Ritual and the Moral Life: Reclaiming the Tradition*, edited by David Solomon, Ruiping Fan, and Ping-cheung Lo, 1–16. Dordrecht: Springer, 2012.

Sparrow, Tom. *The End of Phenomenology: Metaphysics and the New Realism*. Edinburgh: Edinburgh University Press, 2014.

Stalnaker, Aaron. *Overcoming Our Evil: Human Nature and Spiritual Exercises in Xunzi and Augustine*. Washington, DC: Georgetown University Press, 2006.

Tambiah, Stanley. "A Performative Approach to Ritual." *Proceedings of the British Academy* 65 (1979): 113–69.

Taylor, Rodney L. "The Sudden/Gradual Paradigm and Neo-Confucian Mind-Cultivation." *Philosophy East and West*, Vol. 33, no. 1 (January 1983): 17–34.

Thanissaro Bhikkhu, trans. "Nagara Sutta: The City." https://www.accesstoinsight.org/tipitaka/sn/sn12/sn12.065.than.html. Accessed September 2, 2019.

Thanissaro Bhikkhu. "The Truth of Rebirth and Why It Matters for Buddhist Practice." https://www.accesstoinsight.org/lib/authors/thanissaro/truth_of_rebirth.html. Accessed September 2, 2019.

Tu Wei-ming. "'Inner Experience': The Basis of Creativity in Neo-Confucian Thinking." In *Humanity and Self-Cultivation: Essays in*

Confucian Thought, edited by Tu Wei-ming, 102–10. Boston: Cheng & Tsui, 1978.

Walraven, Boudewijn. "Buddhist Accommodation and Appropriation and the Limits of Confucianization." *Journal of Korean Religions* 3, no. 1, Late Chosŏn Buddhism (April 2012): 105–16.

Welter, Albert. *The Administration of Buddhism in China: A Study and Translation of Zanning and His Topical Compendium of the Buddhist Order in China* (Da Song Seng shilue 大宋僧史略). Amherst, New York: Cambria Press, 2018.

Whitehead, Alfred North. *Process and Reality*. New York: Harper & Row, 1960.

Wilhelm, Richard, and Cary F. Baynes, trans. *The I Ching or Book of Changes*. New York: Bollingen Foundation, 1950.

Wilson, Edward O. *The Meaning of Human Existence*. Kindle Edition. New York: Liveright, 2014.

Wirth, Jason. *Nietzsche and Other Buddhas*. Bloomington: Indiana University Press, 2019.

Wolf, Susan. "Happiness and Meaning: Two Aspects of the Good Life." *Social Philosophy & Policy* 14, no. 1 (1997): 207–25.

Wolf, Susan. "Meaning in Life." In *The Meaning of Life: A Reader*, edited by E. D. Klemke and Steven M. Cahn, 232–5. New York: Oxford University Press, 2008.

Wolf, Susan. *Meaning in Life and Why It Matters*. Princeton: Princeton University Press, 2010.

Wolf, Susan. "Meaningfulness: A Third Dimension in the Good Life." *Foundations of Science* 21 (2016): 253–69.

Wong, Peter Yih-Jiun. "Editorial." *Sophia* 51 (2012): 151–3.

Yijing 易經. *Daxu* 大畜. In *Chinese Text Project*, edited by Donald Sturgeon. 2011. https://ctext.org/book-of-changes/da-xu.

Yijing 易經. *Xici shang* 繫辭上. In *Chinese Text Project*, edited by Donald Sturgeon. 2011. https://ctext.org/book-of-changes/xi-ci-shang.

Yijing 易經. *Xici xia* 繫辭下. In *Chinese Text Project*, edited by Donald Sturgeon. 2011. https://ctext.org/book-of-changes/xi-ci-xia/zh.

Zhang Zai 張載. *Hengqu yishuo* 橫渠易說. In *Chinese Text Project*, edited by Donald Sturgeon. 2011. https://ctext.org/wiki.pl?if=gb&chapter=73915.

Zhu Xi 朱熹. *Daxue zhangju* 大學章句. In *Chinese Text Project*, edited by Donald Sturgeon. 2011. https://ctext.org/si-shu-zhang-ju-ji-zhu/da-xue-zhang-ju.

Zhu Xi 朱熹. *Jinsilu* 近思錄. In *Chinese Text Project*, edited by Donald Sturgeon. 2011. https://ctext.org/wiki.pl?if=gb&chapter=149165.

Zhu Xi 朱熹. *Zhuzi yulei* 朱子語類. In *Chinese Text Project*, edited by Donald Sturgeon. 2011. http://ctext.org/zhuzi-yulei/zh.

Ziporyn, Brook. *Beyond Oneness and Difference: Li* 理 *and Coherence in Chinese Buddhist Thought and Its Antecedents*. Albany: SUNY, 2013.

Index

absurdity 15–16, 35, 70, 93, 96, 109–12, 121
alienation 15–16, 96, 112, 115, 121, 132
Ames, Roger 102, 104, 107, 111, 116, 119
Amitābha Buddha 52, 54–5, 62
anagnosis (reading) 97. *See also* reading
anātman (no-self) 45. *See also* no-self
Angle, Stephen C. 109, 124, 139
anitya (impermanence) 45. *See also* impermanence
Aquinas, Thomas 21
authenticity 16, 96, 104, 116–18, 121
authoritarianism 30

Baba, Eiho 5
   zhijue 5, 72–4
Bao Xi 69
Bataille, Georges 41–2, 99, 130–4, 137–8, 140
   Accursed Share, The 42
   Inner Experience 131–5, 137, 140–1
   on nothingness 133–4, 136–8
   restricted and general economies 42–44, 52, 57
Beauvoir, Simone de 4, 43, 117–18, 121
   Ethics of Ambiguity 34
   existential condition 34–6
benxin (original mind) 59. *See also* original mind
benxing (original nature) 59
Bergson, Henri 2, 98
Berkeley, George 26–8, 38
Black existentialism 7
Book of Changes 2, 82. *See also Yijing*
buddhakṣtra (buddha-field) 54

Buddhism/Buddhist thought 7–9, 11–12, 32, 36, 44, 50–4, 57, 94, 123–4, 130. *See also* Chan Buddhism; Mahāyāna; Pure Land; Won Buddhism; Zen
   Eightfold Path 46
   on emptiness and impermanence 8, 114, 135–7
   enlightenment experiences 138
   Four Noble Truths 45–9
   modernist movements 46
   Three Marks 45
buren (inhumane) 110
busi (not thinking) 59
Butler, Judith 13–14, 102–3, 161 n.24, 161 n.29

Cahn, Steven 18–19, 36
Chan Buddhism 58–9, 138
   on emptiness 138
cheng (sincerity) 15–16, 94, 96, 116–21, 136. *See also* creativity; integrity; sincerity
Chinese thought/philosophy/traditions 67, 71, 77, 79, 82, 90–4, 100, 102, 106, 114–5, 127, 136. *See also* Buddhism; Daoism; East Asian philosophies; Ruism
   European nihilism, comparison with 127
   and speculative philosophy 5–6, 12
Christianity and Christian thought 4, 6, 9, 13–14, 99, 143 n.4, 160 n.20
Chu Hsi. *See* Zhu Xi
Clark, Maudemarie 33
commentarial traditions, 84–90
compassion 50, 52

Index

Confucianism 6–7, 15, 100–1, 106, 139. *See also* Ruism
neo-Confucianism 87, 134, 139–140. *See also* Song dynasty; Ming dynasty
Confucius 6, 105–6. *See also* Kongzi
constructivists and constructivism 13, 22, 33, 102
continental philosophy 5, 12, 14, 22, 25
cosmos 9–10, 61, 67, 77–9, 82, 91, 93, 98, 106, 108–10, 119–20. *See also* microcosm and macrocosm; *tian*
creativity 36, 57, 63–6, 74, 94, 99, 116, 119, 122–4, 138, 140–2. *See also* values
 as translation for *ch'angjosŏng* in the work of Kim Iryop 63
 as translation for *cheng* 116–7. *See also cheng*; integrity; sincerity
critical theory 5, 12, 14, 22, 25
Africana 7

dachu (*Yijing* 26th hexagram) 88
daily renewal 15, 88–9, 115
daishi (great death) 138
Daodejing 77, 102, 110
Daoism/Daoist thought 6, 9, 11, 15, 68, 81, 94, 100–1, 125–6
 on absurdity 110–11
 hun and *po*, theory of 74
 meditative practices 80, 115, 124
 on nothingness or emptiness 85, 134–6
 and *qi*-based worldview 77, 79, 130, 134–6
 spontaneity 122–4
daojia/*daojiao*. *See* Daoism
Davis, Bret 145 n.20, 160 n.19, 164 n.86
Daxue (Great Learning) 10–11, 87–8, 118, 121, 127, 132, 139, 146 n.27, 157 n.40, 163 n.70. *See also* Great Learning
death 1, 19, 34, 103, 112

Bataille's view 133–4
and Buddhism 45, 47–50, 54–5, 138
and Daoism 74
Hakuin's "great death" 138
Heidegger's view 104, 108, 117, 137
in the *Guanzi* 80
de (power) 12, 15, 71, 77–8, 81, 111. *See also* power
Descartes, René 4, 26–30
dharma 7
divination 2, 82–4, 90, 105, 126
dualism. *See* subject-object dualism
Dudrick, David 33
duḥka (suffering) 45. *See also* suffering

East Asian philosophies 5–6, 8–9, 11, 14–5, 67–8, 81, 96, 116, 122, 125–7, 130, 141–2
 On emptiness and nothingness 134–7, 138
 on mental energies and subjective interiority 2–4
 and Pure Land Buddhism 53–4
 on ritual and practice 100–1
eko (merit transfer) 55, 62
empiricism 3, 20, 28, 42, 95, 118, 139–40
emptiness. *See also* nothingness; *śūnyatā*; void; *wu*
 in Buddhism 8, 58–9
 in Daoism 85, 135
 debates between Buddhist, Ruists, and Daoists over 125, 134–8, 166 n.19
 in Kim Iryŏp's thought 57–9, 62–3, 65–8, 114
enkrateia (self-mastery) 97
existential freedom 36, 43, 94, 124, 133, 142
existentialism 1–3, 5, 9, 35, 42, 96, 98–99, 102–3, 111–12, 121, 126, 137–38

and cross-cultural work 7, 15, 32, 95–6, 115, 134, 138, 142
key vocabulary of European existentialism 35, 96
and Kim Iryŏp 9, 63, 66
phenomenological approach 3, 17–8, 34–5, 37, 137–8
speculative 5–6, 8, 15–6, 39, 130
extension of knowledge 118–119. *See also* zhizhi

fachulai (manifests outward) 73–4
fa (emits or sends forth) 118
Farquhar, Judith 95
filial piety or family reverence 12, 107, 110, 140
formless/formless *qi* 65, 67–8, 68, 85–7, 114–15, 122, 135–6, 148 n.3. *See also* wuxing
Foucault, Michel 13–14, 22, 97, 99, 102–3, 134, 143 n.4
freedom 16, 24, 35–6, 43, 58, 60, 62, 64, 94, 96, 113, 116–17, 121, 123–4, 133, 142. *See also* existential freedom

Gadamer, Hans Georg 98
Gao Panlong 82, 99
gewu (investigation of things) 118, 163 n.74. *See also* investigating things
Godart, Gerard Clinton 7
goodness 29, 87, 93. *See also* shan
Great Learning 10–11, 87, 89, 118. *See also* Daxue
Gregg, Nina 22
guantong (as integrated awareness) 133
Guanzi 77–80
gua (trigrams) 82–4. *See also* trigrams; hexagrams

Hadot, Pierre 1, 13, 97–9, 142, 143 n.4, 160 n.19
spiritual exercises 1–2, 142. *See also* spiritual exercises

Hakuin 138
Hall, David 111, 116, 119
heart-mind 11, 16, 72–73, 76–77, 81, 86, 88, 109, 112, 115, 129–30. *See also* xin
Zhu Xi on cultivation of 72–3, 76–7, 88, 91, 109, 132–133
he (harmony) 109
he (combine or unify) 109, 120
Hegel, G. W. F. 7, 38–9
Heidegger, Martin 5, 18, 37–8, 42, 103–4, 108, 117–18, 137, 144 n.9
Being and Time 17, 98
being-in-the-world 34
on death-anxiety 105–8
existential phenomenology 17
hexagrams 69, 82–3, 88–9
Hobbes, Thomas 26–8
Hon, Tze-Ki 84–8, 91, 93
Hu Yuan 85–8, 91, 135
huahua (ceaseless transformation) 95
huan (worry) 105
Huineng 59
Hume, David 27–8, 30, 70
hun and *po* 73–4, 77, 79
Hussain, Nadeem 32
Husserl, Edmund 38

impermanence 8, 45, 49, 57, 98. *See also* anitya
Ing, Michael 105–107
inner experience 8, 14, 16, 28, 127, 129, 140–2. *See also* interiority; mental energy
Bataille's views on 131–4, 137, 140–2
Tu Weiming's views on 140–2
integrity (in the sense of *cheng*) 116, 120. *See also* cheng; creativity; sincerity
interiority 2, 5, 16, 127, 129, 134. *See also* inner experience; mental energy
inner life and outer world 2–3, 8, 14, 57, 64, 72, 90, 92, 121

investigating of things 10, 88, 118.
    See also gewu
is–ought problem 90

jia (family or lineage) 6
jing (seriousness) 15, 94, 96, 108–10.
    See also seriousness
jingshuang (essential and refreshing) 75
jing (stillness) 15, 94, 96, 112–13. See also stillness
jingtu (Pure Land) 54. See also Pure Land
jingzuo (quiet sitting) 76, 115
jinxing (completing nature) 120
junzi (exemplary person) 105–6, 139

Kaibara Ekken 135–6, 138, 166 n.18
Kant, Immanuel 21, 28–30, 33, 37
    Critique of Pure Reason 17
karma 42, 45, 48, 49–51, 55–57, 61–7, 115
    Buddhist analysis 45–50
    karmic economy 8, 42, 44–8, 56–7, 125
    definition 45
    existential theory 56–8
    Iryŏp's view 58–67
    merit 2, 8, 42, 44–5, 48–56, 61–2
Kim Iryŏp 9, 52, 58–9
    on creativity and value creation 62–7, 74, 120, 124, 138
    on emptiness 57–9, 62–3, 65–8, 114, 136, 138
    ideas of non-duality 64, 66–7
    on karma 61–2, 67
    on "life energy" or "life force" 64–5, 67–8, 125–6
    on meditation 7–8, 11, 41–2, 65–7, 81, 114–15, 123–6
    monasticism 58, 66, 131
    on "mind of nothingness" 58–9, 63

social and political activism 60–2, 66, 86
Kim, Yung Sik 75
Klossowski, Pierre 131
Kongzi (Confucius) 6, 105–7, 122.
    See also Confucius
Kopf, Gereon 138, 166 n.22
Kundera, Milan 69–70, 93, 109
    Unbearable Lightness of Being, The 69
Kyoto School 138, 160 n.19

Langsam, Harold 32
Lazzarato, Maurizio 12
li (ritual) 100, 102, 104, 108, 112. See also ritual
li (structure) 9–12, 71, 76–8, 80–1, 118, 120, 139. See also structure
life energy 64–5, 67, 125–6, 136. See also saengmyŏng; shenming
Liji (Book of Rites) 10, 87, 95, 104–107
ling (numinosity) 11, 75, 91. See also numinosity
literati 6–7
Liu, JeeLoo 91, 96, 134–7, 141, 143–4 n.6, 157 n.38, 158 n.46, 158 nn.50–1, 165 n.15
    on nothingness 134–7, 141
Locke, John 26–8
Lunyu (Analects) 105, 145 n.14

Mahāyāna 52–4, 57–8, 61–3, 65, 136, 166 n.19
materialism 3, 90. See also new materialism
materiality and the question of dualism 9, 14, 27, 30, 71, 77, 98, 99, 143 n.4
matter-energy matrix 68, 71–2, 76, 111, 142, 142 n.6. See also qi
meaning 1–5, 14–6, 26, 30, 39, 70–1, 92, 142, 143 n.4, 145–6 n.21
    Bataille, Georges 42–5

Beauvior, Simone de 34–6, 66
Buddhism 11, 56
Cahn/Wolf debate 18–20, 29
Daoism 11, 110–11
Farquhar and Zhang 95
Kim Iryŏp 57, 62, 66–7
Heidegger, Martin 17–8, 42, 103–4, 117
Nietzsche, Friedrich 15, 31–3, 43, 66
qi-based worldview of Ruism 11, 93–4, 108, 111, 121, 124, 126–7, 129–30, 141
Wilson, E. O. 23–4, 29
Yijing 81, 83–5, 88
meditation
   Gao Panlong on 82
   Kim Iryŏp on 65–7, 81, 114–15, 123–6
   power of 8, 65, 105
   Ruists views on 97, 99–101, 105
   trans-egoic power of 8, 14
Meillassoux, Quentin, *After Finitude* 37
meletai (meditation) 97. *See also* meditation
memorization 2, 73, 75–7, 98–9, 101. *See also mneme*; scholar/scholarship
mental energy/mental experience 3–4, 16, 71–2, 74–78, 115, 119, 129–30, 139
   mind-*qi* 12, 75, 119
merit. *See* karma
metaphysics 3, 5, 16, 17, 29, 96, 98, 103, 117, 121, 134, 143 n.4, 144 n.10, 145 n.19
   morality and metaphysics in Chinese thought 91–3, 111
   and the question of nothingness 68, 85, 135–6, 141
   and realism 33–4, 36, 38, 92
   and subjectivity 2–4, 14, 20, 30–1, 37, 99, 102, 117, 129

microcosm and macrocosm 2, 9, 10, 71, 77–8, 80, 83, 88–9, 105, 108–9, 112, 119, 121, 130
mind. *See* heart-mind, inner experience, interiority, and mental energy
Ming dynasty 9, 82, 97, 109, 135
mneme (memorization) 104. *See also* memorization
monotheism 25, 127, 131
mysticism/mystical experience 99, 129, 131–3, 143 n.4, 148 n.3

Nelson, Eric S. 151 n.17
new materialism 5, 37
Nietzsche, Friedrich 1–2, 8, 13–15, 22, 35–6, 63, 66, 84, 94, 98–9, 142, 147 n.35
   psychological writings 74
   Thus Spoke Zarathustra 31
   value-creation 30–4, 81
   will to power 126. *See also* will to power
nihilism/nihilist 4, 19–20, 32–3, 36, 110, 125, 127, 135–6, 138
no-self 45, 49, 57. *See also anātman*
nothingness 67–8, 86–7, 135–138, 141. *See also* emptiness; *śūnyatā*; void; *wu*
   Bataille on 133–134, 137
   Kim Iryŏp on "mind of nothingness" 58–9, 63
   Liu, JeeLoo on 134–7, 141
   Sartre on 113–4
numinosity/numinous 11, 75, 91, 94. *See also ling*

objectivity 20–2, 26, 33, 90, 147 n.35
object-oriented ontology 5, 37
original mind 59, 62, 64, 66. *See also benxin*

Pāli canon 47
Park, Bradley 123–4

Park, Jin Y. 60, 152 n.32, 153 n.43
Parkes, Graham 15, 32, 143 n.5,
    147 n.37
  comparative works on Nietzsche
    99, 126
  Composing the Soul 74
perception 5, 27–8, 72, 92. *See also*
    zhijue
phenomenology/phenomenologists
    3–5, 16–18, 20, 28, 34, 36,
    39, 98–9, 102, 126, 129, 134,
    137–8
  criticism of 18, 36–9
  Kant on phenomena 28–9, 33,
    37–8
Plato 4, 92, 97
Poellner, Peter 33–4
power. 11–12, 71, 82, 89, 106, 121,
    123–4, 127, 141. *See also de*;
    will to power
  in Daoism and the *Guanzi* 77–8,
    80–1, 110–111
  in the *Daxue* 10, 87–88
  Iryŏp's ideas 8, 40, 59, 62–6, 131
  of the mind/mental powers 46,
    80–1, 113–15, 121, 127, 131,
    139–40
  political 71, 85–8
  of the sage 15, 75, 78
  of self-cultivation 16, 88–9, 130
  social context 12–13, 22, 101–2
pratītyasamutpāda or "dependent
    origination." 47
prosoche (training of attention) 97
puṇya (merit) 48. *See also* karma
Pure Land 53–6. *See also* Ch. *jingtu*
    (Pure Land)

qi 9–10, 14–16, 73–4, 79–81, 90–5,
    116, 120–1, 125–6, 131, 138,
    142, 137. *See also* matter-
    energy matrix
  formless 68, 86–7, 114–15, 122,
    135–6
  and inner experience 16, 129–30
  mind-*qi* 12, 75, 119
  primal or primordial 68, 79–81,
    85–6, 94, 115–16, 120, 122,
    135
  qi-realism 91–2, 96
  Zhang Zai's views 86–7, 93
  Zhu Xi's views 76–7, 91, 119
qing (phenomenological quality)
    81
qin (loving) 88

rationalism 3–4, 14, 28–9, 34, 90, 160
    n.19
reading 82, 84, 86, 88, 95, 97,
    118, 121, 139–42. *See also*
    anagnosis; scholar/scholarship;
    Zhu Xi
realism/realists 3–5, 22–3, 26, 28–30,
    34, 37–9, 71, 90–2, 96, 113,
    127
re-habituation 2, 16, 39, 96–7, 100,
    103
ren (humaneness) 110
res cogitans (thinking thing) 4, 30
res extensa (extended thing) 30
rixin (daily renewal) 15, 109. *See also*
    daily renewal
ritual 16, 97, 99
  in Buddhism 8, 52–3, 55, 100–1,
    125
  ritual efficacy 101–3
  in Ruism 7, 95, 100–12, 115, 121,
    127, 139. *See also li* (ritual)
Rosemont, Henry 102, 104
Ruism/Ruist thought 7–9, 11–12,
    67–8, 75, 79–82, 87, 91, 94,
    97, 99, 118, 120, 124–6, 131,
    139. *See also* literati; scholar/
    scholarship
  on anxiety 104–8, 112, 117
  criticism of Daoism 85, 135
  criticism of Buddhism 135,
    137–40

on emptiness or nothingness 125, 134–8, 166 n.19
on absurdity 109–12
radical existentialism 124–6
ritual 7, 95, 100–12, 115, 121, 127, 139. *See also li* (ritual)
on seriousness 109–12
rujia (scholarly lineage) 6. *See also* literati; scholar/scholarship
ru (scholar or literati) 6

saengmyŏng (life energy) 64, 67, 153 n.53. *See also* life energy; *shenming*
sage 11–12, 15, 75–6, 78–81, 119, 138–9, 139, 142
Śākyamuni Buddha 45–7, 54, 56, 145 n.16
Sartre, Jean-Paul 38, 102, 112–14, 117, 121
on nothingness 112–14
satori (enlightenment) 138
scandal of philosophy 17–18, 37, 39
scholar/scholarship, Ruist 6–8, 10, 82, 90–1, 101, 105, 140
scholar-apprentices 139
scholarly methods 16, 97, 99
scholar-officials 85
self-cultivation 11, 13–14, 16, 78, 95, 130–1
Ruist view 86–7, 89, 97, 105, 109, 115–16, 121, 139
selflessness 49–51, 62. *See also anātman*; no-self
self-transformation 2, 12, 76–9
seriousness 15, 94, 96, 108–12, 115, 121, 126, 139–40, 142. *See also jing*
shan (goodness) 93. *See also* goodness
Shaviro, Steven 5
shengming ("life energy") 67, 153 n.53. *See also* life energy; *saengmyŏng*
shengren (sage) 11, 75, 139. *See also* sage

shengsheng (ceaseless renewal) 15, 95
sheng (vitality) 67, 80–1. *See also* vitality
shenhui (spiritual communion) 141–2
shenming (spiritual clarity) 11, 69, 75
shen (spirit/spiritual) 73, 75, 119. *See also* spirit/spiritual
shi (scholar-apprentices) 139
shōsuru (actualization) 138
shunli (following *li*) 120
Siddhartha 46
silu (deliberative thought) 91
sincerity 15–16, 94, 96, 116–17, 119–21, 124, 126, 136. *See also cheng*; creativity; integrity
skepsis (investigation) 4, 9, 21, 23, 30, 34, 39, 71, 97, 114, 118, 134
solicitude (*you*) 15, 94, 96, 105–6, 108, 112, 126. *See also you*
solipsism 26, 28, 36–7, 39. *See also* Descartes
Song dynasty 5, 8, 10, 71, 84–5, 108, 126, 135–6, 139
Sorge (concept of care) 104–5
Sparrow, Tom 38
speculative existentialism 5–6, 8, 15–16, 39, 130
speculative philosophy 4, 12, 38, 117, 121
in Chinese thought 95, 108, 126
speculative realism 5, 37
spirit/spiritual 9, 14, 73, 75, 119. *See also shen*
spiritual exercises 1–2, 97–9, 131, 142, 160 n.19
Greek and Roman 1–2, 14, 97, 143 n.4, 145 n.19
spontaneity 15–16, 94, 96, 116, 121, 123–4, 126. *See also ziran*
St. Ignatius Loyola 131
stillness 11, 15–16, 77–8, 94, 96, 113–15, 121, 126. *See also jing*
structure 2, 9–14, 16, 76–81, 83, 88–9, 92, 105–6, 109, 130. *See also li*

Index

structural tendencies 71, 108, 112, 118, 120, 137, 142
structural change 65–6
subjectivity 12–13, 26, 30, 90, 121, 137, 140, 142. *See also* interiority
subject–object dualism 2, 4, 19–20, 30–2, 34, 36, 58, 66. *See also* interiority
Sudŏk Monastery 64
suffering 45–50, 54, 56–8. *See also* duḥka
Sukhāvatī (Amitābha's buddha-field) 54, 62. *See also* Amitābha Buddha
śūnyatā (emptiness) 136, 166 n.19. *See also* emptiness; nothingness; void; *wu*

taiji (Supreme Ultimate) 135–6
taixu (Great Vacuity) 86
Thanissaro Bhikkhu 48–9, 151 nn.12–13
Theravāda 52
tian (cosmos) 9–10, 61, 67, 77–9, 82, 91, 93, 98, 106, 108–10, 119–20. *See also* cosmos
tian di zhi xin (heart-mind of the universe)
ti ("body" or "embodiment") 141
trigrams 82–4, 89. *See also gua*
Tu Weiming, 140–2, 167 n.29
    'Inner Experience': The Basis of Creativity in Neo-Confucian Thinking 167 n.29

values. *See also* creativity; metaphysics; Nietzsche
    creation of 14, 30–4, 36, 42, 62, 67, 81, 84, 116, 142
    realization of 71, 85, 90–3
    Ruist views 109–10, 125–6
vitality 15, 80–1, 142, 153 n.53
vitalism 3
void/voidness 59, 68, 79, 85. *See also* emptiness; nothingness; *wu*; śūnyatā;

wei (doing) 123
Western thought/philosophy 2–5, 12, 15, 18, 20–1, 26, 30, 35, 92, 95–6. *See also* metaphysics; realism; subject–object dualism
    is-ought problem 90
    and the question of practice 2, 13, 16, 97, 99–101
Westernization/Eurocentrism 6–7
Whitehead, Alfred North 5, 102–3
will to power 15, 31–2, 124. *See also* Nietzsche
Wilson, E. O. 24–5, 29, 43
wisdom 46, 57, 110. *See also zhi*
Wirth, Jason 145 n.20, 164 n.86
Wolf, Susan 18–20, 25, 29, 33
Won Buddhism 125
wu (emptiness) 7, 47–8, 50, 54, 57, 68, 85–7, 100, 127, 136, 138–9. *See also* emptiness; nothingness; śūnyatā; void
wunian (no-thought) 59, 123
wuxi (ceaseless) 121
wuxing (formless) 68, 85, 87, 136. *See also* formless

xiaoren ("small" or "petty" people) 11, 75, 115
xiaoxue (lesser learning) 139
xin (heart-mind) 11, 72, 77, 88, 91. *See also* heart-mind
xinzhai (fasting the heart-mind) 80, 115
xuexi (studying and learning) 118
Xunzi 139

Yijing (*Book of Changes*) 2, 81–90, 105, 123, 126, 135, 141. *See also Book of Changes*
yin and *yang* 73–4, 77, 81, 83, 86, 108, 111, 122, 125
yi (righteousness) 15, 110, 118
you (existence) 86–7
you (solicitude) 15, 94, 96, 103–6, 112. *See also* solicitude

youxing (formed/having form) 85, 87
yu (desire) 118

zazen (seated meditation) 100
Zen 56, 58, 100, 126, 138
zetesis (research) 97
Zhang Qicheng 95
Zhang Zai 86–9, 91, 93, 157 n.38, 158 n.45
zhijue (perception) 5, 72–5, 77, 79, 91–2. *See also* perception
zhi (wisdom) 91, 110, 120. *See also* wisdom
zhizhi (extension of knowledge) 118. *See also* extension of knowledge

Zhu Xi 10, 71, 78, 86–87, 126, 135
    on mental cultivation 72–3, 75–7, 88, 91, 109, 127, 132–3
    on memorizing and reciting texts 76–9
    on reading 76, 118, 126, 140–1
    on studying and learning 118–9
ziran (spontaneity) 15, 94, 96, 116, 121, 123–4. *See also* spontaneity
zuowang (sitting and forgetting) 115

www.ingramcontent.com/pod-product-compliance
Lightning Source LLC
Chambersburg PA
CBHW070639300426
44111CB00013B/2178